# THE
# PATTERNS
# OF EASY
# INFLUENCE

―――

―――

——

---

---

————

——

———

———

———

———

———

# THE PREAMBLE

---

**THE STRANGEST SECRET – FOREWORD**

Let me tell you the strangest story and the strangest secret. I have a vivid memory of this moment burned into my head. My mind always wanders back to it. It's the moment everything changed. I'll tell you exactly what happened. Then I'll tell you exactly why this changes everything about persuasive presentation, compelling communication, and powerful public speaking.

I was a college student when it happened. Much of my life since has been spent developing the single critical insight that slapped me in the face one fateful day.

Let's begin.

I was watching reruns of Bill Clinton's debate against Bush. Why? Because I'm odd like that. I'm fascinated by public speaking and communication; so fascinated that I ended up winning 32 awards as a competitive public speaker, coaching hundreds of mentees, and winning national speech competitions.

And in this particular moment I was feeling a little nostalgic for my competitive debating days. So that's

---

why I was watching Clinton's most compelling debate moment while I should have been in Microeconomics class. I analyzed every single word, intonation, and gesture. Every single muscle shift in his facial expression meant something specific and, to me, strategically selected for a particular impact.

I'll admit something shameful. I was cocky. I was arrogant. I thought I knew everything there was to know about public speaking.

I thought every technique Clinton used was something (1) I had already discovered, (2) I had already used as a competitive public speaker, and (3) I had already written about in my first book, *How to Master Public Speaking*.

And I had good reason to think so! Need I reiterate my public speaking accomplishments? I won't, I'll spare you; just know I'd be happy to list them out again. The point is this: I was arrogant and felt like I knew everything there was to know about public speaking.

―――

Inclusive pronouns like "we," which put him and his audience on a team, fighting for the same cause together? Check. Knew about them. Used them. Wrote about them.

Portraying both empathy and authority, the qualities of a true leader? Check. Knew about them. Used them. Wrote about them.

Narrow-eyed eye contact with the head tilted slightly up to create captivating intensity, and outward gestures to draw the audience in? Check. Knew about them. Used them. Wrote about them.

So far, this was all old news. But as I watched Clinton speak, I realized an incredible secret. Something so big, so obvious, and so powerful, but at the same time so subtle, secret, and hidden, that my brain couldn't completely process it. I re-winded the video. One more time. A third time. A fourth.

Trust me on this: I don't like not knowing things. And in this moment, I realized that there was something so incredible that I hadn't known all this time. Talk

―――

about getting knocked down a few pegs. It's okay: I needed it (and probably still do). Pride cometh before destruction, and a haughty spirit before a fall.

Just one problem. Bill Clinton was a single data point. A very interesting data point, but a lonely one. I needed to know if I had stumbled upon the motherload or not. I needed to know if this was just a passing accident or a deliberate, intentional, and accessible example of a secret that would revolutionize communication theory.

Turns out it wasn't just a passing trend.

Video after video.

Transcript after transcript.

Speaker after speaker.

From Martin Luther King, to Bernie Sanders, to JFK, to Barack Obama, to Ronald Reagan, to Mahatma Ghandi, to Hillary Clinton, to Donald Trump, and hundreds of other famous speakers, I saw what I saw in Bill Clinton repeated again and again.

But more significantly, I've gone through example after example of failed speeches. Speeches that fell flat. Speeches that didn't motivate. Speeches that lacked power. Speeches that were, in a word, "meh." And not only did successful speeches consistently use this secret, the unsuccessful ones consistently did not.

Like I said, I don't like not knowing things. And for someone who has had as much experience as I have on the subject of public speaking, and who has written about 25 books (as of today) on the subject, it was sobering. I realized, in a swift moment, that I didn't know 80% of public speaking, like I thought, but only 20%. And the worst part? That 20% wasn't even the most important stuff.

But as dismayed as I was, I was also excited. Thrilled, even. Why? Because I found something new. I went online and searched diligently to see if anyone else discovered what I discovered that fateful day. And to be truthful, some other people have stumbled upon it. But only the tip of the iceberg. And if you stick around, I'm going to give you the whole damn iceberg, from top to bottom. Let me tell you this: it's a *massive* iceberg.

Why should you care? Because this secret will take the anxiety out of public speaking. This secret will make persuasion easy. This secret will make presentations *50% done for you before you even start*. This secret can be used in presentations, public speeches, meetings, conversations, writing, you name it. If it's communication, this secret will revolutionize everything you thought you knew about it.

I bet you want to know the secret. Are you still reading this right now? If so, it's because this introduction itself was an example of the secret in action.

Now, let me tell you the big secret. In a word, just a single word, *which means the difference between failed and successful communication*, and in a gross oversimplification of what I've discovered, here's the powerful, hidden, little-known secret: *structure*.

In this book, you will learn everything I've discovered about this secret. I hold nothing back.

This secret will revolutionize your communication, which will revolutionize your life.

And here's the best part: I present to you not only what I've learned, but how I've learned what I've learned, and how I've created what I've created.

You'll see what I mean by "created."

And how will that help you? You'll be able to take advantage of the secret in an extremely specific way, tailored exactly to your life, and your communication needs. Why? Because I'm not only giving you what I've built with the tools of this theory, but the tools themselves.

So, I want you to join me in building out this secret in your own life, and reap the incredible fruits of doing so. Sound fair enough? Keep reading if you're interested.

## THIS IS THE BEST PART

I'm a public speaker at heart. That's my background. But the best part of this secret is that it works with all types of communication. Writing, speaking to one person, *anything*. I want you to remember this as we go on: *if it's communication, these strategies work*. The reason I tell you this now is because I portray these ideas through the lens of giving a presentation or a speech, and sometimes speaking to a single person. But the scope of these ideas is limitless. They directly translate to writing too, for example. Just a side-note before we move on.

## WHY YOU SHOULD TRUST ME

I owe it to you to explain my credentials. You can decide if I'm trustworthy or not.

I was the Massachusetts Speech and Debate League State Champion. I won 32 awards as a competitive public speaker. I was the champion of eight different state-wide speech competitions. I coached hundreds of successful competitive public speakers. I won national speech competitions. I spent days (yes, until there were dark circles under my eyes and the fourth coffee didn't help with my sleepiness) analyzing political speeches and the famous speeches of history. That's where I first

———

discovered this secret. I saw first-hand, when I worked in the Massachusetts Statehouse, the communication and persuasion techniques of senators and representatives. I saw this secret in action there too. I received a seal of special distinction from the National Speech and Debate Association. I have read countless books and scientific articles on communication and audience psychology. I had a speech impediment as a child, and it can still be heard today. I coached Toastmasters national finalists, mayoral candidates, and one of the country's top project managers.

# CHAPTER ONE
# THE THEORIES

## MODELS OF COMMUNICATION

Most people don't know the basic theories of effective communication. This is deeply unfortunate. The one covered in this book, "structure-theory," is just one of many. And it'll make more sense to you, and be more useful, if we support it with the context of some other theories.

Just remember two things. First, there are *many* more communication models than these. We are just going through the most relevant ones. Second, we are going wide, covering a lot of theories, but not deep into each theory.

I suspect that by the end of just these 29 theories, you will be a drastically better communicator, you will avoid common communication mistakes, and you will be able to persuade with ease and confidence.

## 1.1: THE PUBLIC SPEAKING TRIAD

I coined this as the public speaking triad. But, in truth, it should be called the communication triad. The theory

———

goes like this: for all communication to succeed, the communicator must connect to the receivers of the communication and to his or her message, the receivers must connect to the communicator and to his or her message, and the message must connect to the communicator and to the receivers. Everything else about communication comes down to the foundation of this single concept.

Let me put it more simply: for successful communication to occur, the communicator(s), the receiver(s), and the message(s) must all connect. Each one of those three must be connected to the other two. If any one of the connections breaks, the entire communication fails and falls apart.

In the context of public speaking, for a persuasive speech, the speaker must connect to the message to draw upon a reserve of emotional energy when communicating, and the speaker must connect to the audience to understand their pre-existing beliefs, pain-points, and mental states (plus much more which we will get to in short order). The audience must connect to the speaker so that they can meet their trust thresholds, and the audience must connect to the idea by seeing it as relevant to their lives (maybe a solution to a problem, for example). And finally, the idea must connect to the speaker, because the speaker must have some compelling stake in the idea, and thorough knowledge of it (plus the ability to convey this knowledge), while it must connect to the audience because, if it is not relevant to them, they won't care about it.

One last key: the connections usually grow together, and usually fall together. If you improve one of the connections, the others tend to follow suit immediately. I call this the "rising tide" effect.

## 1.2: THE COMMUNICATION TOOLBOX AND THREE-LAYER COMMUNICATION

How do you build the public speaking triad? Think about it: you know exactly what you need to accomplish for your communication to succeed. So, how do you do it?

It depends on the medium. In writing, you have only words, which means you can fully apply structure theory since it deals with just words.

But when speaking, you have words, body language, and your voice. In other words, you aren't communicating with one language, but three. You have the language of your words (English, for example), the language of your body, and the language of your voice. Right now, I'm communicating with you just with my "word language." If I were speaking to you in a lecture-hall, or a seminar, or a training, I would be using three languages: words, body, and voice.

If you go through the free video course you get as part of this book, I'll communicate with you through my voice and word languages (but not body language, since the backgrounds are slides). The course is available at www.publicspeakinghub.com/video-course.

———

So, to summarize, the public speaking triad is the three-way connection between speaker, audience, and message, and you build it with your words, body language, and vocal tonalities. Sound good so far?

And here's a huge secret for you: the vast majority of communication advice deals with this theory alone. Any "tip" or piece of advice you receive has to do with empowering your words, body language, and voice in some way.

Think about this book, which teaches you exactly how to organize your words for maximum impact. Which part of the public speaking toolbox does it deal with? Which of your languages does it empower? Your words. I'll throw you some examples of tips that fall under each of the languages, just to strengthen your understanding.

For your word language, use "secrecy" phrases, like these: "secret," "hidden," "little-known," "never-before-seen," "classified," "unknown," "forbidden," "underground," etc. These secrecy phrases build

———

mystery and intrigue, and play into natural, innate human curiosity. "Security" phrases are powerful too: "proven," "guaranteed," "time-tested," "scientific," are four examples. There are so many different categories of words that impact your audience in different ways. These are just two of them. See how these types of words strengthen the speaker to audience and idea to audience connections?

For your body language, use open body language. What's open body language? Simply put, open body language is when you open your torso, face your audience, and keep your hands out in plain sight. This open body language is a symbol buried deep into our subconscious psychologies by evolution, and it communicates that "this person can be trusted!" See how this improves the speaker to audience connection?

For your vocal language, use breaking-rapport tonality. This is when the pitch (and if you want, pace and volume) of your voice go down at the end of your statements. These make you seem confident in yourself

---

and your ideas. They also signal and create a sense of "conclusion." The sharper the breaking-rapport, the more conclusive and believable a statement sounds. See how this improves the speaker to audience connection?

There are *thousands* of techniques that fall under each of the strategies. They are rooted firmly in human psychology. Why does technique X produce effect Y in humans? Because our psychologies have evolved that way. And overriding human psychology is not something people can easily do, even to themselves, which is why these strategies are so damn powerful.

You'll learn plenty of these strategies in this book; strategies falling under the "word language" bucket. You'll learn a few hundred in my other book, which fall under each of the three buckets. And, in my future books, you'll learn thousands more. Who knows? Maybe I'll even discover a fourth language (I'm considering visuals as one, as in presentation slides, but I'm not sure if it counts. It's like Pluto: not quite a planet, but not something we can ignore either).

---

## 1.3: ACTIVATION, CONTROL, ALIGNMENT

You're aware, at this point, that you have three languages when you're speaking, and that you use them to create a three-way connection between three elements: the speaker, the audience, and the idea. By my estimation, you're already ahead of 90% of other people at this point.

Let me throw you another trifecta: your three languages must be all *activated*, all in your deliberate *control*, and all in *alignment* with one another. If these three conditions are not met, your communication will not be effective. In other words, it won't accomplish its purpose (more on this later). But what do activation, control, and alignment mean? Let's dive into this theory.

Activation: your three languages must all be activated.

Control: your three languages must all be in your deliberate control; in other words, you must be able to say to yourself while you're communicating that, "If I do X with [insert language], effect Y will happen to my

———

audience." You must be confident in this, and you must also be able to actually do X, whatever technique it might stand for.

Alignment: once you activate your three languages, once you bring them under your deliberate control, you must bring them all in alignment. In other words: the three ways human beings convey meaning must be conveying the same meaning.

Think about it: if a speaker is speaking confident words, with a confident voice, but is portraying total insecurity with their body language, are they communicating effectively? Nope. Not a chance. Why not? Because their three languages are not in alignment.

Imagine another scenario: a speaker is speaking engaging words with engaging body language, but a monotone vocal tonality. What happens? If you've ever listened to this type of communication, you already know. The audience tunes out.

Misalignment ruins the speaker to audience connection. Why? Because the audience doesn't

———

necessarily trust words alone. People can easily manipulate their words. The audience then looks to two other languages which are not easily manipulated: the voice and body languages. If these two align? The trust threshold is passed (for most people, under most circumstances). If not? The connection is instantly harmed. In fact, this is why some cite the statistic that communication is only 7 percent verbal and 93 percent non-verbal. The non-verbal component is made up of body language (55 percent) and tone of voice (38 percent).

Let's say you are communicating through a medium where you only have two languages. They must still be in alignment.

Let's say you're writing, and have one language: that one language better be activated and in your control, although it has no other language to align to.

Now, I mentioned this previously: I said "Your communication will not be effective. In other words, it won't accomplish its purpose (more on this later)." Later is now. Let's talk about purposeful communication, right after we wrap up the triad by identifying some key ingredients of each connection.

## 1.4: TRIAD INGREDIENTS

Here's the truth about the triad: each of the connections are strengthened by a set of characteristics.

Speaker to audience: the speaker can help the audience, the speaker can provide a solution to the audience's problem, the speaker understands the audience.

Speaker to idea: the speaker thoroughly understands the idea, the speaker has an incentive to spread the idea, the speaker believes in the idea.

Audience to speaker: the audience trusts, knows, and likes the speaker, the audience sees the speaker as an authority figure, and the audience feels that the speaker has empathy for them and understands their pain.

Audience to idea: the audience believes the idea has value to them, the audience finds the idea to be a solution to a problem, and the audience trusts the idea.

Idea to speaker: the idea has impacted the speaker's life in a significant way (or the speaker has impacted the idea's life in a significant way, as an expert does for the ideas in his field).

Idea to audience: the idea is relevant to the audience's life (or the audience is relevant to the idea's life, as is the case for an idea that the audience must help spread).

Remember: while these characteristics are essential, they are just some of the ingredients that make up the connections in the triad.

## 1.5: PURPOSEFUL COMMUNICATION

Communication can be confusing. Trust me, I know. But I promise that it doesn't have to be that way. If you understand and use purposeful communication in your writing and speaking, communication will instantly become something you enjoy. And here's the best part:

purposeful communication is, in its simplest form, just a mental model of how to view communication. But don't be fooled: it's an incredibly in-depth and diverse area of communication theory. We are just covering the simple components of this theory right now.

It goes like this. All communication (at least, all communication worth engaging in) must have a purpose. Communication is effective if it fulfills that purpose. Communication is not effective if it does not fulfill that purpose. There is a "starting state," which describes the world before your communication. There is a "finishing state," which describes the world after your communication, if its purpose has been fulfilled. In truly purposeful communication, every single word, sentence, paragraph, structural component, pause, vocal intonation, gesture... or, in other words, *every single use of your three languages,* must be specifically, strategically, deliberately designed to move in a straight line from the starting state to the finishing state.

And don't take "straight line" to necessarily suggest a forceful, direct approach lacking all measures of subtlety or nuance. Why? Because, sometimes, and probably most of the time, the straightest line (that is, the most effective path), from starting state to ending state, is one that contains subtlety and nuance.

Does the foundation of this theory make sense to you? Every action you take when you're communicating, as this theory dictates, must be designed to move the world closer to your desired outcome.

When I edit speeches or persuasive writing, I run through this following process for cleaning, simplifying, and empowering language. This process is informed by the theory of purposeful communication. First, take a sentence you're editing, or the first one in the speech. Identify the one purpose of that sentence clearly (in a sentence, perhaps) as it relates to your one overarching purpose. Go through each word, phrase, etc., and decide if it helps towards that purpose, or detracts away from that purpose. If it does help, does it help enough to justify keeping it when keeping it dilutes the power of the other stuff that potentially helps more, or if it takes the place of another unit of meaning that would help more? Remove detractors, keep helpers. Repeat for next sentence. Repeat multiple times if you'd like, slowly chiseling to perfection.

Of course, there's a "step zero" to this process, which is to identify a worthwhile purpose in the first place.

In *The Way of the Wolf*, author Jordan Belfort describes a similar theory of persuasive communication in this way: "On the straight line, directly on it, every single word, every single statement, sentence, *everything* is fulfilling the open to close purpose. No free words, no time for stupid statements, no time to go off to Pluto and talk about the price of tea in China. Being in-control, specifically directly on the line, is directed, powerful; your words have meaning, and the meaning is to create massive certainty in the audience's minds. Every word has a purpose."

If your communication doesn't have a purpose, then don't communicate. It's that simple. But if it does have a purpose? You better make sure every single use of your three languages moves you towards fulfilling that purpose.

## 1.6: THREE-PART MODEL

This one is, well... pretty damn obvious. And it is fundamental to structure theory.

Here it is: all communication has three parts. A beginning, a middle, and an end.

Obvious so far, right? Technically, everything has a beginning, an end, and a time in between the beginning and the end that we label as the middle.

But you must remember that each of the three parts has its own distinct goals. This is the basis of structure theory. Let's break down an example of this into a hierarchy of structures.

Level one structure: **beginning** – get attention in a way that is relevant to the content of the speech, **middle**

— close the gap between starting state and finishing state, and **end** — ensure that the audience follows through on creating the finishing state.

Level two structure: **beginning**: <u>APP</u> — establish empathy, authority, and create curiosity, middle: <u>DDD trifecta</u> — create a strong desire in your audience to perform your suggested action, ending: <u>SBA</u> — end on a note most likely to create high audience follow-through.

Level three structure: **APP**: **a**gree — create empathy, **p**romise — portray authority, **p**review — create curiosity and a mental "open-loop," **DDD trifecta**: **d**esire — make your audience want a certain thing, **d**issonance — show your audience how they are missing what they desire and create cognitive discomfort, **d**ecision — suggest the necessary decision that will realize the desire and end the dissonance, **SBA**: <u>summarize</u> — re-cement the factual information in your audience's minds to create logical certainty, <u>benefits</u> — repeat the tantalizing benefits to set you up for the next step, <u>action</u> — describe to your audience the action you want them to take.

See how we filled in the "beginning, middle, and end" with those weird-looking formula things? See how those weird-looking formula things broke down into sub-structures, with distinct steps that fulfill secondary purposes? See how the secondary purposes ultimately come together to fulfill the primary purpose? These funny formula things (APP, DDD, SBA, and about 40 other ones) are what you learn in this book.

Are you confused? I would be surprised if you weren't. Just know this: throughout this book, you'll learn the exact, proven, step-by-step structures to use for 90% of your communication.

In other words: instead of seeing persuasive communication as a confusing soup of random statements, you'll see it as an organized, orderly set of structures that clearly move the world from its starting state to your chosen finishing state. Sound fair enough? That's the awesome power that the theory of structured communication gives you. I won't break this all down this instant: that's what the whole book is for.

## 1.7: CONE OF ATTENTION

Here's the theory: every single audience has a set of subjects that results in them narrowing their attention to only focus on you (if you communicate about these subjects). This is "top of cone" communication, near the vertex of the cone, where its volume is smaller; where it is *narrower*. If you speak about these "top of cone" subjects, your audience will narrowly focus on you. Think about it: a cone is narrower at the top. It includes less things, and if you're lucky, the cone of attention will be so narrow it only includes you. But it has nothing to do with luck, and everything to do with deliberately chosen messages.

On the flip side: every single audience has a set of subjects that, if you speak about them, will completely dilute their attention away from you. These are "bottom of cone," where its volume is larger; where it includes more things, and not just you.

Here's where it gets tricky: there is no universal cone.

———

Here's were it gets simpler: there is a sort of universal vertex.

Imagine a bunch of different cones overlapping only at the top, flaring out in different directions but meeting in a shared vertex.

You're probably wishing there was some sort of universal cone; that there was some sort of universal key unlocking every single person equally, and grabbing everyone's attention to the same degree.

Well, don't despair: the core psychological human desires are that key. If you speak about the core human desires, you will almost always be "top of cone," and your audience — and almost any audience — will give you their narrow attention.

If you speak without invoking the core human desires, that's a problem. You'll be "bottom of cone," and you won't earn undivided attention.

That said, every single audience has a different cone. In other words, they want different external things, but they want those different external things (the body of the cone) because they satisfy the same core desires (the overlapping vertex of the cone). A financier on Wallstreet wants to hit the next hot stock to satisfy the same desires (emphasis on the plural) as a fisherman in East Asia seeking a full net of seabass. Different *means*, yes, but to the same *ends*.

Let me put it this way: many of us want the same things, but we go about achieving those things in different ways. There are means (what we want to achieve) and ends (why we want to achieve those things). While the means differ wildly, the ends are often very similar. They are a set of core human desires and needs.

Why am I telling you this? Because of the cone of audience attention, of course. If you know your audience's means and ends, invoke them both. You'll be right there near the vertex of the cone. If you don't know the means, then identify the ends and invoke those. That will get you very close, and here's the key: because most of these core desires are widely shared, they are the unifying point for diverse cones of attention; they are

———

——

where different cones of attention, flaring out in different directions and belonging to wildly different people, meet.

Now, what I'm about to tell you is a whole new theory, but I'm lumping it closely to this one. How do you identify the core desires at play? Use the "many-fold-why."

Here's an example: a financier wants to hit the next hot stock. Why? To make money. Why do they want more money? To afford nicer things, and to feel financial security. Here we branch.

The "nicer-things" branch: why do they want to afford nicer things? To have a more attractive outward appearance. Why do they want that? For social status and prestige. Bam! You've isolated two core motivating desires of that financier.

Now the "financial security" branch: why do they want financial security? To be safe no matter what happens. Why do they want that? To be free to do whatever they want, and free from fear. Bam! Two more.

——

———

Guess what? Now we know the exact subjects that will make an audience of financiers (and probably fishermen too) listen in. We have the exact, core, psychological human desires that will immediately take you to the "top of cone," where effective communication happens because its prerequisite is met: attention.

Remember this: social status, prestige, freedom to act, and freedom from fear are all key motivating desires that (most likely) describe why the fisherman wants a full net. In part, at least. What's *inherently* valuable about a bunch of flopping fish trapped in a rope net in the middle of the ocean? Nothing. Sure, the fisherman can eat some of them, but not all of them without getting Mercury poisoning. It is only valuable because it fulfills the deeper desires of the fisherman.

Want to know why someone does something? Look at the impacts of their action. It's that simple. You'll find that the wide and infinite array of diverse human action often boils down to satisfying the same core desires,

———

———

which is where disparate and diverse cones of attention belonging to disparate and diverse people meet.

You bought (or borrowed or stole) this book because you want to be more influential. What could give you more influence in communication than what I just told you? Not a whole lot.

## 1.8: THE RIGHT THINGS THE RIGHT WAY

Here's a secret: *your words are important, but so is how you look and sound saying them.* We talked about your three languages. This theory is an extension of that theory.

Everyone can say the right things. Only a person who is confident and authentic can say the right things in the right ways.

There are those who manipulate themselves and inauthentically say the right things in the right ways, and they are those who can't say the right things or say them in the right ways no matter what. Don't be either of those people.

———

Here's the truth: your words impact your audience consciously and subconsciously. They inherently pass the traffic-stop of the conscious, logical, analytical mind on their way to the audience subconscious. At this traffic stop, their influence is dulled, and they often arrive at the subconscious mind a quivering shadow of what they once were, if they weren't rejected and sent away. Structure theory and certain uses of language are designed to bypass this intrinsic limitation. More on that later.

But guess what? Your body language and vocal tonalities skip that traffic stop. They are a one-way-street with a 120-mile-per-hour speed limit, taking you directly to your audience's subconscious minds. And which mind has more power over someone? The subconscious one, which researchers estimate makes up between 70% and 94% of our mind.

Can you imagine someone thinking, "I disagree with this idea because [insert reasoned, conscious objection]?" Of course you can. It happens all the time. This is the conscious filter acting on words.

Can you imagine someone thinking, "This speaker is engaged, authentic, and wearing a big smile; he is loud, confident, and self-assured; he is presenting eye-contact, using vocal emphasis appropriately, and gesturing with intent. As a result, I think his point is compelling." Or, on the flip side, can you imagine someone thinking, "This speaker is engaged, authentic, and wearing a big smile; he is loud, confident, and self-assured; he is presenting eye-contact, using vocal emphasis appropriately, and gesturing with intent. I am going to ignore this when judging his point?" I can hardly imagine either of them occurring in the real world, because these characteristics of the speaker – unlike most (but not all) of the speaker's words – pass the conscious filter. They are largely subconsciously perceived, and so is their impact on audience cognition. The advantage of this? It passes the skepticism that sometimes, and often, but not always, characterizes the conscious filter. Understand?

I want you to remember this when we talk about the theory of "additional words." I'll remind you if you forget. But this theory forms the basis of that theory. See how these are all interconnected building-blocks?

## 1.9: SELF-INTEREST AND "WIIFM?"

I read a lot of books about psychology, communication, the psychology of communication, influence, leadership, people-skills, persuasion, sales, and anything else in this intriguing web of subjects. I study and write about them, so it's nice to see other perspectives.

Why am I telling you this? Here's why: *because there is such an extremely unanimous consensus on what I'm about to tell you.* I mean a truly extreme consensus. Every single book in this web of subject agrees on this.

Here is the truth: if you want to communicate with persuasion and influence, appeal to people's self-interest and answer the question "what's in it for me?" or "WIIFM?"

If you do this, you have their attention and interest. If not? You don't have their attention, or their interest, and you most definitely are not going to communicate effectively. In other words, you most certainly won't move from starting state to finishing state.

Why? This has to do with the next two theories (ten and eleven). I want you to remember this: all of this is baked directly into our mental makeup as human beings. Evolution put it there. That's why these bedrock theories are so powerful.

## 1.10: PERCIEVED MARGINAL BENEFITS, PERCEIVED MARGINAL COSTS

This one is so foundational and fundamental to effective communication that you cannot miss it. Let's get right into it.

Why must you follow theory nine (self-interest and WIIFM?) Here's why: because of this equation.

If you ever took a Microeconomics course, like the one I was skipping when I discovered structure theory

———

way back in college, you're familiar with the marginal benefits versus marginal costs equation.

Energy in, energy out, is the same as marginal benefits versus marginal costs.

These theories (which are really the same thing) go like this: if someone perceives the marginal benefits of an activity to be greater than the marginal cost (including the value of the alternative activity forgone), all else equal, they will do that activity until the marginal benefits begin to be eclipsed by the marginal costs. If the costs exceed the benefits, they won't engage in an activity.

Energy in, energy out: if the energy someone has to put into an activity is greater than the rewards they get out of that activity, they won't engage in it.

Marginal benefits > marginal costs = activity engaged in until marginal costs > marginal benefits.

Marginal benefits < marginal costs = activity not engaged in until marginal costs < marginal benefits.

Keep in mind the essential key of applying this theory: this has nothing to do with actual benefits and

———

actual costs, and everything to do with *perceived* benefits and perceived costs.

And this is exactly how this theory links to self-interest and WIIFM. When you speak in terms of self-interest and answer the question "what's in it for me?" then perceived marginal benefits (or energy out) seem higher and higher and yet still higher than perceived marginal costs (or energy in).

Get it? Now, you might be asking "what activity are they engaging in? What does this have to do with persuasive communication and applying persuasive communication patterns?" Here are your answers: the activity they are engaging in (if you properly balance this equation by addressing self-interest and WIIFM) is listening to you; it is opting-in to give you their attention and mental space. Those are resources, *scarce* resources, that you are implicitly asking them to give up to you. You better make sure they think what they get by giving up the resources to you is greater in value than the resources themselves.

———

As for question number two, "what does this have to do with persuasive communication and persuasive communication patterns?" the answer is... everything. If you don't get them to opt-in to receiving your communication with enthusiasm by showing them, implicitly and explicitly, that marginal benefits far exceed marginal costs, then you don't get their attention and brain-space, which means you can't persuade, because you can't truly communicate. Sure, you can *try*, but nobody will really be there to receive it. They'll be running through a to-do list, day-dreaming, or thinking about a totally unrelated subject, all while pretending to listen to you.

And this links perfectly to our next theory of eight seconds and the mental checklist, which then links to structure theory.

Before we get into that, know this: the further benefits exceed costs, the more enthused and attentive your audience will be. On the contrary, the further costs exceed benefits, the less enthused and attentive your

———

audience will be. Yes, there is a *threshold* where marginal benefits are greater than marginal costs, but there is also a *spectrum*: the more marginal benefits exceed marginal costs, the more attention you get.

## 1.11: EIGHT SECONDS AND THE MENTAL CHECKLIST

A quick recap (since you're probably confused, *since this stuff is confusing at first*): to communicate persuasively and achieve a purpose with communication, you must make sure that your audience perceives the benefits of listening to you to be higher than the costs of listening to you. And to do that, you must speak in terms of their self-interest, and answer the WIIFM question. All good so far.

Here's how those theories link to this theory: how do people decide if benefits of listening exceed costs of listening? By running through a mental checklist.

How quickly do they run through the mental checklist after you begin speaking? In about 8 seconds.

So not only do you have to express that energy out is greater than energy in by invoking self-interest, but you also have to do it quickly.

That's definitely a daunting task. I won't pretend it isn't. But it will be significantly easier for you than it is for others. Why? Because in this book, you learn structures acting as strategically designed templates for meeting the mental checklist, balancing the energy equation, and portraying immense value, and doing so quickly.

That's power. That's easy power. That's immediate power. That's addictive power. All you have to do to instantly get almost anyone's attention is to take one of these proven language patterns, plug in your words, and say the damn thing.

That's good news, isn't it?

The rest of the book will be these exact persuasive patterns and structures. Right now, we're just getting into why they work, and the bedrock theories that support them.

---

## 1.12: BENEFITS, BENEFITS VERSUS FEATURES, AND CONFUSION

This goes back to self-interest and the energy equation. Let me give you a brief run-down of this theory.

Benefits are the positive outcomes your audience will experience as a result of listening to you or taking your suggested action.

Features are what create the benefits. What about your suggested action will produce those benefits? Those elements are the features.

Benefits versus features, and confusion, describe the following question (and debate): when you want to speak in terms of self-interest and tip the energy equation in your favor, what do you speak in terms of? Benefits, or features?

This is a deeply divisive question in marketing and advertising, although a consensus has begun to emerge. What sells more? The benefits of a product, or the features that produce those benefits?

---

---

And in reference to persuasive communication, what appeals to people's self-interest more? What makes perceived energy out higher? Benefits, or features?

The truth is this: speaking in terms of just features is the worst, and speaking in terms of just benefits is okay. But luckily for you, you don't have to pick one. It's a false dilemma.

The best case is this: speak in terms of both features and benefits. How? By either describing a feature, and then explaining the benefits of that feature, or by starting with benefits, and then explaining the features that create them.

And believe me: this has nothing to do with products in a "Life-cereal," "Coca-Cola," or "Chevy truck" sense of the word, but in the sense of ideas, which are a different kind of product people sell and buy. It's called the "marketplace of ideas" for a reason.

Want some examples of this in persuasive communication? Here's a political one (I love politics). I

---

italicized the audience's internal monologues in reaction to each of the statements.

Features only: "This healthcare plan will decentralize the planning of aggregate treatments, and instead use blockchain and feedback infrastructure to determine what treatments to enact and when to enact them." *[What does that soup of big complicated words even mean? I have no idea what this politician is trying to say. Can't he just tell me how this will impact my life? I really don't trust him anymore, and I have no faith in this healthcare plan because I don't know what it means for my life.]*

Benefits only: "This healthcare plan will make you pay less money and receive better treatment." *[Woah! That sounds great. I see how that will impact my life. I definitely would love to pay less money. That's a huge plus. And I need better treatment. But it's just a promise. Can I trust it? It sounds good, but will it really happen? I'm doubting this. I'm intrigued, but not fully on-board.]*

Features and benefits (which produce a similar internal monologue as benefits first and features second): "This healthcare plan will decentralize the planning of aggregate treatments, and instead use blockchain and feedback infrastructure to determine what treatments to enact and when to enact them, which will make the whole system less wasteful and more efficient *[a bridge statement, which we'll get into later]*, and therefore make you pay less money and receive better treatment." *[I'm blown away! I definitely would love to pay less money and receive better treatment. This is perfect. And what a well-thought-out plan! It makes perfect sense. I know exactly how this will impact my life, and exactly how it's going to work. I trust this guy and his plan. I'm going to donate to his campaign and vote for him!]*

When you're promising benefits to someone, they want to believe you. But without explaining the features that create those benefits, they can't. And if your features are particularly complex, throw in a bridge statement to connect your features to your benefits in a believable and understandable way.

Now, let's move on to a wonderful parable.

## 1.13: THE WIND AND THE SUN

This one secret of persuasion and influence in communication will completely change everything you thought you knew about this subject. *Completely*. It comes to us in the form of a parable passed down over thousands of years.

The North Wind and the Sun had a quarrel about which of them was the stronger. While they were disputing with much heat and bluster, a Traveler passed along the road wrapped in a cloak.

"Let us agree," said the Sun, "that he is the stronger who can strip that Traveler of his cloak."

"Very well," growled the North Wind, and at once sent a cold, howling blast against the Traveler.

With the first gust of wind the ends of the cloak whipped about the Traveler's body. But he immediately wrapped it closely around him, and the harder the Wind blew, the tighter he held it to him. The North Wind tore angrily at the cloak, but all his efforts were in vain.

Then the Sun began to shine. At first his beams were gentle, and in the pleasant warmth after the bitter cold of the North Wind, the Traveler unfastened his cloak and let it hang loosely from his shoulders. The Sun's rays grew warmer and warmer. The man took off his cap and mopped his brow. At last he became so heated that he pulled off his cloak, and, to escape the blazing sunshine, threw himself down in the welcome shade of a tree by the roadside.

The moral? Gentleness and kind persuasion win where force and bluster fail. We'll revisit this shortly.

## 1.14: MENTAL MALLEABILITY

This is something you *must* understand if any of the techniques, persuasive patterns, and strategies in this book will work for you.

Remember when we talked about purposeful communication? Remember how we talked about a starting state and a finishing state? If not, go back and reread that (shame on you!) If yes, keep reading.

Here's the truth: persuasive communication, by its very nature, revolves around creating a desired finishing state in the world, which has to do with your audience taking some action. It might be buying a product, implementing a plan, thinking a new way, or doing anything that creates your desired finishing state in the real world. Good so far?

At this point, this theory comes into play. Here it is: for every single finishing state that revolves around your audience taking some action, there is a particular mental state which will immediately make them more likely to take that action. Make sense? For every action X, there is a mental state Y which will make people more likely to take action X. But this is just part one of the theory.

Part two is this: people have mental malleability; in other words, outside influences and inputs will change their mental state.

See where I'm going with this? In summary: for every action you want your audience to take, there is a particular mental state which will make taking that action more likely, and that mental state can be induced by outside inputs, including your communication.

So, to give you a clear process that you can use to instantly apply this theory, I broke it down into these steps: first, identify what action you want your audience to take. Second, identify what mental state will make them most likely to actually take that action. Third, use the principle of mental malleability, and communicate the persuasive inputs to your audience that will mold their mental state to the one most likely to create your desired action.

It's that simple. Three simple, easy steps to instantly make your audience more likely to take your desired action.

But don't get me wrong: I'm not, for a *second*, pretending like step three is easy. It's not easy at all, unless you prepare yourself with the knowledge of your public speaking toolbox (remember that?). In other words, step three becomes easy only if you understand this: "If I use my [word / body / vocal] language in

———

[insert way], then that input will produce the following impact on my audience's mental state: [insert impact]."

That's tough, but as you begin to unlock your public speaking and communication toolbox and understand persuasive cause and effect, it becomes much easier.

## 1.15: BRIDGE THEORY

This builds off the theory of purposeful communication. Let me restate the theory of purposeful communication. All communication (at least, all communication worth engaging in) must have a purpose; communication is effective if it fulfills that purpose; communication is not effective if it does not fulfill that purpose. There is a "starting state," which describes the world before your communication; there is a "finishing state," which describes the world after your communication, when its purpose has been fulfilled. In truly purposeful communication, every single word, sentence, paragraph, structural component, pause, vocal intonation, gesture… or, in other words, *every single use of your three*

———

———

*languages*, must be specifically, strategically, deliberately designed to move in a straight line from the starting state to the finishing state.

Doesn't it follow logically that, if all effective communication must have an overarching goal, this overarching goal can be broken down into sub-goals that all add up to the total goal?

Of course it does. And here's the truth: if you are truly communicating efficiently (which is engaging, persuasive, and captivating), then you must be able to point to each and every statement you make, and identify a clear purpose for that statement, and not only a clear purpose, but a clear purpose that moves the communication towards accomplishing your overall goal.

Get it? But that's not quite it, because you need to connect these "purpose statements" in some way. How? With bridges, or transitions.

So, following this theory, if you are speaking from a script, you should be able to point to every single

———

statement and say "this statement accomplishes a clear purpose, and that clear purpose moves the world from my starting state to my desired finishing state, thereby completing my ultimate purpose" or "this statement or clump of words is there to connect and transition from one purpose statement to another."

If you can't say either of those two things about part of your communication, you should carefully consider removing it.

## 1.16: THE HUMAN DESIRE PYRAMID

Remember the cone of attention? Remember self-interest and WIIFM? This theory relates to those. Well, in truth, *all* these theories relate to *all* these theories.

Here's this theory: all humans have a set of core, innate desires; we desire other desires to satisfy our core desires; we desire other desires to satisfy the desires that satisfy our core desires; we desire other desires to... continued endlessly.

Confused? Let me explain. We have thousands of desires. Some of those desires are core, and other desires are manifestations of those core desires.

We have desire X, and then because of desire X, we have desire Y, because desire Y satisfies desire X. And then because desire Z satisfies desire Y, we want that too. And, so on and so forth.

In summary: we have a set of core desires, and from those core desires emanates a massive pyramid of desires which are all linked because they satisfy other desires. Let's revisit our financier who wants the next hot stock: "A financier wants to hit the next hot stock. Why? To make money. Why do they want more money? To afford nicer things, and to feel financial security. Here we branch. The 'nicer-things' branch: why do they want to afford nicer things? To have a more attractive outward appearance. Why do they want that? For social status and prestige. Bam! You've isolated two core motivating desires of that financier. The 'financial security' branch: why do they want financial security? To be safe no matter what happens. Why do they want that? To be free to do whatever they want, and free from fear. Bam! Two more."

Core desires: social status and freedom.

Level one derived desires: a more attractive outward appearance, and to be safe no matter what happens.

Level two derived desires: affording nicer things, and financial security.

Level three derived desires: more money.

Level four derived desires: hitting the next hot stock.

The core desires at the top of the pyramid are more likely to be shared by others. Everyone (almost everyone) shares the desires of high social status and freedom. Not everyone shares the desires of hitting the next hot stock. As you move further down the pyramid, into tertiary desires (and even further), you begin to reach a place where the desire set is more and more unique to your audience.

And check out this conflict: we branch into "affording nicer things," and "financial security" at level

———

two of the desire pyramid. The more you satisfy the "nicer things" desire, the less you can satisfy the "financial security" desire. Get it? Much human indecision and internal conflict has to do with having two conflicting desires (as this financier does) and not knowing the degree to which to satisfy each. Further, much human motivation derives from having conflicting desires and seeking to reach a point of abundance where the sheer magnitude of resources renders the conflict meaningless.

And here's a key lesson: every person has different derived desires, similar core desires, and a different value hierarchy; in other words, they place their desires in different hierarchies of value.

This flows directly into the next few theories of persuasive communication.

———

___

### 1.17: AUDIENCE UNIQUENESS, AUDIENCE PERSONAS, LIMITS OF THEORIES, AND CETERIS PARIBUS

This is a chunky theory. There are four parts to it that all tie together. Let's take them one by one.

Part one, audience uniqueness: no audience is the same. They all have different human desire pyramids and value hierarchies. They all come with their own needs, beliefs, values, objections, pain-points, preconceptions about you, hierarchy of values, past experiences with similar ideas, speakers, and situations, and much more. To quote again from *The Way of the Wolf:* "We all arrive at any particular moment in time with a history of beliefs and values and opinions and experiences and victories and defeats and insecurities and decision-making strategies – and then based on all of that stuff, our brain, working at near light speed, will instantly relate it to whatever scenario lies before it. Then, based on the result, it will place us at whatever point on the certainty scale it deems appropriate for each of the three tens, and

—

it's from that starting point that we can then be influenced."

Part two, audience personas: based on your pre-existing intelligence, and the intelligence you can gather, you can develop a "persona" that includes the previously mentioned characteristics and describes at least two-thirds of your audience. Now you know who you're speaking to. Let's say you are having trouble creating an audience persona: let's say you have a broad audience, with a wide variety of different kinds of people. What do you do then? Build your persona around what unites them. And speak in terms of core human desires, engaging with their self-interest as it exists at the top of the human desire pyramid, where most people have similar desires (remember the diverse cones with overlapping vertices)?

But what if you're speaking to a group of people you can identify as relatively homogenous? What if you can build a clear and compelling audience persona that is distinct, specific, and in-depth? What if you can clearly

—

___

identify audience needs, beliefs, values, objections, pain-points, preconceptions about you, hierarchy of values, past experiences with similar ideas, speakers, and situations? Then make *that* the audience persona. In this case, you can engage with your audience's self-interest at all stages of the human desire pyramid. If you're speaking to financiers, you know they all are likely to share a human desire pyramid that looks at least something like what we identified earlier.

Core desires: social status and freedom.

Level one derived desires: a more attractive outward appearance, and to be safe no matter what happens.

Level two derived desires: affording nicer things, and financial security.

Level three derived desires: more money.

Level four derived desires: hitting the next hot stock.

And, in this case, you can safely engage with them at all five levels of desires.

Part three, limits of theories: no communication theory is bullet-proof in every situation. No

___

communication theory works for every audience, under every circumstance, for every speaker, for every situation, for every subject. It just doesn't apply. The real world is too messy. We can't predict every lurking variable. Now, we know this: in the vast majority of cases, these theories work. But these theories, due to the infinite variety of human psychological states, and the infinite variety of possible externalities, are only effective if our assumptions about first, human psychology, and second, externalities, are correct. But here's the good news: the vast majority of the time, our assumptions about these two things *are* correct. That said, we, inevitably, arrive at a necessary caveat to this (and all) social theories. We discuss it now, in part four of this theory.

Part four, the *ceteris paribus* assumption: if you have explored any social science, like economics, politics, or psychology, you have knowingly or unknowingly stumbled across this assumption. *Ceteris paribus* is Latin for "other things equal." And all of these theories are

---

bullet-proof only under this assumption. For example, Monroe's Motivated Sequence (which I will teach you) is a proven speech structure that, other things equal, makes you much more likely to persuade your audience. Understand?

Now, you might be wondering, "what use are these theories if we have to apply that assumption?" Here's my answer: *think about gravity*. If we drop a feather and a brick from the same height, according to the law of gravity, they should arrive at the ground at the same time. Go ahead and try it! You'll see that the feather falls much slower than the brick. Is the law of gravity broken? No. It's just air resistance. But here's my point: the law of gravity requires the ceteris paribus assumption too. It requires removing all external variables and isolating the relationship between the two variables you want to study. If the law of gravity requires this assumption, we can safely say it's reasonable to apply it for social theoies as well.

---

———

These theories, if you remove all external variables, will make you infinitely more persuasive, basically instantly. But if you're speaking to a room of ten people who all hate you on a deep, personal level, are these theories going to work? They'll make you more persuasive *than you would have otherwise been,* but they won't outweigh that external variable of deep hatred towards you and create an easily measurable difference in outcome.

In what we traditionally think of as science, you can isolate the relationship between two variables easily with a test-tube. You can't do the same with the social sciences. That's why this assumption is necessary. Even with gravity, you can remove the impact of air resistance by creating a vacuum.

A brief side-note: sorry for putting that "ten people who hate you" thought into your head. I'm sure you're wonderful, and that no matter how hard I tried, I couldn't find ten whole people who dislike you.

———

Anyway, let's move on to our next theory which builds off of audience uniqueness and audience personas (but also ties into self-interest, benefits, and the human desire pyramid).

## 1.18: SALIENCY, INTENSITY, STABILITY

Here's how this theory connects to audience uniqueness and the idea of audience personas: first, build an audience persona; second, identify the subjects that are salient, intense, and stable to that audience persona; third, speak in terms of those subjects.

Let me explain. Every single statement has three qualities: saliency, intensity, and stability. Every statement has these qualities in varying amounts, and the most compelling statements have the most of all of them.

Saliency refers to how many people care about a given subject, or in other words, how important a given subject is. It is the portion of the population that cares about something.

Intensity is a measure of how strongly people care about a subject. It is a measure of how much energy people are willing to devote towards one topic.

Stability is how long people are willing to continue caring about a given subject, or how easy it is to switch the opinions of those who already care about a given subject (the harder it is to change their minds, the more "stable" their points of view).

In summary, saliency is how many people care, intensity is how much they care, and stability is for how long they will care.

Because saliency, intensity, and stability are not intuitive concepts, here's another helpful way to think about them: saliency is how important a topic is, intensity is how important it is to those who think it's important, and stability is for how long it will be important to those who think it's important.

Every compelling subject or statement is salient, intense, and stable. By combining these three qualities, you can maximize the chance that what you're saying will have an impact on your audience and that they will tune in; that it will be "top of cone."

In many cases, however, your topic might not be salient, intense, or stable. In this situation, the best strategy is to find the most salient, intense, and stable *consequences* of what you're speaking about and deliberately connect them to your subject.

Everything of impact occurring in the real world has consequences and is connected to other occurrences. Many topics are part of an interconnected web, in which everything impacts everything else in one way or another.

By tapping into and connecting your subject to another one which is more salient, intense, and stable, you gain the very useful benefit of speaking in terms of something which most people in your audience will care about, which they will care about strongly, and which they will continue caring about long after you finish your speech. Stability is particularly important: stability is essentially the longevity of concern, interest, or relevance your ideas have to your audience. If they only care about what you're saying when you're saying it, and not after or even before you've said it, that's obviously a big disadvantage. Avoid this by connecting your idea to something you know your audience will care about in the long run.

As any career politician will vehemently assert, the economy is one of the most salient, intense, and stable issues. It's not the highest in any of the categories but, on balance, its average rating is probably at the top. People will vote for a candidate who has a disappointing personal track record if they believe that he or she will lower their taxes. People love money. It's that simple.

It might make you cynical to think that money is high on the list of what people care about, but it shouldn't. It makes sense that it is, so use it to your advantage.

Think of these three qualities as a three-way Venn diagram. In other words, think of them as three circles that each overlap each other. Something can be in only one circle, in two circles, or in the center where they all

---

overlap, and where it is enclosed by all three circles. The more circles your subject and theme are enclosed by, the more interested in your speech your audience will be. If your subject either ends up in the middle of that diagram, or you can find a logical connection that brings it there, then your persuasive power will be maximized.

### 1.19: ONE VERSUS MANY

This theory directly addresses the specific techniques you learn in this book, and the thousands of techniques that are all different ways of using your three languages.

Remember what these techniques really are. When I tell you to "do X with your body language," or "do X with your voice," or in the case of this book, "do X with your words," it's me telling you to "provide input X to your audience, *to create result Y.*"

And here's the tricky part: the causation relationship between X and Y is not always clear, for two reasons, namely incomplete feedback and external variables.

---

Let's talk about incomplete feedback. When I tell you to use one of these speech structures, for example, you're not going to have people walking up to you saying "Oh wow! Great structure, the reason I'm buying this product you're selling is because of that structure. Great use of your word language! It really persuaded me." You just don't get that type of instant feedback. And it gets trickier: *your audience doesn't even always know what persuaded them.* Sometimes they do. But even if you did get people making these kinds of statements, there would be no reason to believe them with certainty. They don't always know how the techniques impacted them, and in what ways. The more subtle the technique, the less likely the audience detected it, and vice-versa. If, for example, they tell you about a particular piece of information they valued highly in their judgement, or a particular logical argument you made, you have more reason to trust that this was in fact the persuasive factor that influenced them (or one of the persuasive factors, at least).

———

———

And now let's talk about external variables (again): when I tell you to "provide input X to create impact Y on your audience," that doesn't mean that you aren't also providing thousands of other inputs which all tip the scale in one of two ways. In other words, no one technique will make the key difference; instead, persuasive communication succeeds because the aggregate, summed-up total of your inputs are persuasive. It's possible that one technique brings you over the edge, but only because it's standing on thousands of other inputs. I guarantee that these structures you will learn are incredibly powerful, proven persuasive language patterns. I do not guarantee that these structures will outweigh 200 other wrong inputs you might provide to your audience. I guarantee that they will tip the scale in your favor, but not so much that they will outweigh anything tipping the scale against you.

And these two considerations create this theory: because persuasion is not the result of a single input, but the result of the summation of all your inputs, the impact

———

of a single technique is not going to guarantee persuasive success. One does not outweigh many.

But rejoice: 20% of the actions are particularly powerful, and produce 80% of the results. In other words, 20% of your persuasive inputs in communication produce 80% of the persuasion. The structure of persuasive communication is a big part of that 20%, which acts as a powerful lever with serious impact on the persuasive scale. Sound fair enough?

## 1.20: PSYCHOLOGICAL PERSUASION

Persuasion occurs in the mind, not outside of it. Persuasive communication is trying to influence a mind to believe something. This probably seems insanely obvious, but here's the point: you do not convince anyone; you simply apply the theory of mental malleability to get them to convince themselves. It all occurs in *their* minds.

Thus, we turn to the theory of psychological persuasion. Since persuasion occurs in the mind of the

_____

*receiver* of communication, this means that the environment of the receiving mind, or the psychology of it, is inherent to persuasion. And now we arrive at the final principle of this theory: *things are persuasive because of human psychology.*

In other words, effective persuasive communication is effective because it uses the characteristics of human psychology in its favor. Get it?

Let me give you an example. Remember the APP opening structure from the three-part-communication theory?

Why does it work? What makes it effective? What makes it persuasive? What makes it move the world from starting state to finishing state? Why is it different from other communication beginnings?

Here's the answer to all those questions: it uses the characteristics of human psychology in its favor.

How? Here's how: the APP opening, in one of its forms, is starting your persuasive communication by

_____

agreeing to an audience pain-point, promising a solution, and previewing that solution.

Think about the characteristics of human psychology that this opening uses to grab attention and set the stage for successful persuasive communication.

Agreeing portrays empathy, and empathy is the foundation for trust. We will be persuaded by those we trust. Why? Psychology.

Agreeing to a pain-point will draw attention to and emphasize the struggle and pain related to it, which is the precursor to action, because we want to escape from and relieve pain. We will be persuaded when our struggles are top-of-mind. Why? Psychology.

Promising benefits portrays value, and high perceived value is the foundation for receiving attention (which you need if you're going to persuade). We will be persuaded by someone who we see as valuable to us. Why? Psychology. (Remember energy in, energy out?)

Promising also portrays benefits and a solution to a problem. This appeals to self-interest and whichever core human desires are harmed by the problem. We will be persuaded by someone who appeals to our self-interest, because we think they can help us get what we want. Why? Psychology.

Previewing creates a giant mental open-loop. Curiosity tantalizes us, particularly in the context of the APP method (because of the empathy, trust, and high value portrayed so far). A giant mental open-loop, or in essence, a massive unanswered question, grabs our attention and makes us want the answer. We will be persuaded when we are captivated by curiosity. Why? Psychology.

The same holds true for every single structure and persuasive pattern you learn in this book.

If you're ever wondering "why does this work?" remember the answer: psychology.

## 1.21: SPEAKING FOR ACTION

Why do we speak? What does it mean to try to persuade someone? How do you know if you have succeeded? We

———

speak to get people to take action. When we persuade successfully, that action is taken.

But it's not that black and white. If you want someone to buy something you're selling, and they don't, that doesn't mean you've totally failed at persuasive communication. Why? Because, what if they go on to talk about your product to twenty friends, who then buy it? Maybe you didn't persuade them to buy it themselves, but you persuaded them to have faith in your idea and to see it as something that will serve some of the people they know. Get it? Just remember that persuasion is not binary: it's a spectrum. If you move *closer* to your desired finishing state, even if you don't get all the way there, or if you accomplish a *related* purpose, even if it wasn't your primary goal, then the persuasion made your reality better. Thus, it can be considered a success.

And one more thing: energy in versus energy out applies to your call to action too. Got it? There are two times when you most need to maximize the energy out

———

and minimize the energy in: at the start, and when you call your audience to action. Why? Because these are the two major points where you are actually asking you audience to do something. And they only will if you properly balance that equation.

## 1.22: 7C (OR 14C) COMMUNICATION

It's funny: business schools love applauding this concept and teaching it to their students as the 7Cs of communication. According to me, they leave out seven additional Cs. In truth, it's more like 14Cs.

What are the original 7Cs? Clear; concise; concrete; correct; coherent; complete; courteous.

And the second 7Cs? Creative; contextual; credible; compelling; consistent; connected; and coherent again (because most people miss this one...)

## 1.23: NOVELTY AND SIMPLICITY

This ties to the energy in energy out theory. Let's get into it. Effective communication has two key characteristics:

novelty and simplicity. In other words, you must be providing rapid-fire *new* information in a *simple* way.

Let's start with novelty: as Donald Draper, the main character of the highly acclaimed show *Mad Men* once said, "the most important word in advertising is *new*." In public speaking, a powerful gift from you to your audience is something new: something unfamiliar to them, and something you haven't already told them. Everyone appreciates the speaker who gives them the most comprehensive information, especially if it is new and can give them a competitive advantage in life.

Our attention spans (on a micro-scale) have apparently dropped from 12 seconds to eight since the dawn of the internet age. So, if there's one lesson public speakers can gain from electronic media such as YouTube videos and Instagram feeds, which have experienced astounding success at gaining the attention of a global audience, let it be this: present new and exciting information rapidly.

As for simplicity: there's beauty in simplicity. An idea presented simply is an idea long remembered by your audience. Focus on the big picture before getting into specifics, and make sure that your audience is following the progression of your speech.

Oftentimes, experts forget that they are speaking to an audience that isn't made up of other experts. What ensues is a situation in which the speaker describes things in the complex jargon of his or her trade, while the audience is left helplessly trying to follow along. If you are presenting a complex topic, don't make your audience feel like they are "mentally running" to keep up with you. Hold their hands and take them for a nice, gentle walk through the information instead.

Break down your speech until it is simple and easy to follow. Unless you are aiming for evocative, flowing, beautiful language, don't say more than you need to. Furthermore, don't say it in more complex words than you need to. Always keep it simple.

———

Why does it link to the energy equation? Because receiving simple information is perceived as lower-cost. It truly is lower-cost: less mental energy is required to receive simple communication, because of its simplicity, than complex communication. As for novelty, while simple information decreases energy in, rapid-fire information increases energy out. In other words: rapid-fire simple information seems more valuable than slow information, and it also reduces the energy expense.

Get it? We're almost done before we get to structure-theory. Stay with me. You already, because of this section, have a much stronger understanding of persuasive communication than the vast majority of people. And this will make the rest of the book so much more useful to you.

———

___

## 1.24: UNCERTAINTY VERSUS CERTAINTY, EMOTIONAL VERSUS LOGICAL, SPECTRUMS, ATTENTION, AND COUNTERFACTUAL SIMULATION (AKA MENTAL MOVIES)

Remember the theory of mental malleability? Remember how there is one particular mental state that will almost force your audience to take your suggested action? Remember how, through strategic persuasive inputs, you can induce that mental state in your audience? Let's build on that with this multi-part theory.

Part one, the idea of spectrums: if you really want to successfully apply the theory of mental malleability, you have to take one extra step and boil down mental states into spectrums. In essence, spectrum theory goes like this: your desired mental state, the one you want to induce in your audience through inputs, can be broken down into a series of qualities, each of which with their own spectrum of magnitude. Thus, with your persuasive inputs, or your action-levers, you can move people up

---

and down these spectrums to achieve the desired mental state.

For example, let's say you're a politician campaigning for votes. What is the mental state that will most likely make your audience take the action you want them to, and bring about your desired finishing state?

Let's think about it. It goes much deeper than this, but for the sake of example, here are the qualities of that ideal mental state: anger towards the other party, belief in personal gain as a result of voting for you, connection and agreement on values, and connection and agreement on policy.

Now, think of it this way: for each of these qualities, your audience can be at a one level, or a ten level. At ten, they completely have the quality. At one, they completely lack it. Get it? So, to achieve persuasive communication, your communication must be geared at moving your audience from wherever they start on these spectrums to wherever you want them to be. Your statements should be geared towards making them angry towards

———

the other party (moving them towards a ten – the most possible anger), showing them their personal benefit of voting for you (moving them towards a ten – the highest possible perception of benefit), and connecting on values and policy (moving them towards a ten – the deepest possible connection). And this is just one simple example of a mental state broken down into a set of qualities. The examples are infinite. I can't possibly predict what yours will be, but (like I just did) I can equip you with the tools to figure it out and use the theory for yourself. And think about the theory of purposeful communication: how do you know if a statement is contributing to or diluting from your persuasive communication? Ask yourself if it manipulates one of these spectrums in your favor or not.

Part two, attention and certainty: while each ideal audience mental state can be broken down into a vastly unique set of qualities, every single ideal mental state must have some basic ingredients. Let's break them down. Your audience must be close to a ten on the

———

———

attention spectrum, close to a ten on the trust in you spectrum, close to ten on the trust in your idea spectrum, and close to ten on the trust in the group you represent spectrum. So, let's update your ideal audience mental state, most likely to result in action: they must be close to a ten on whatever spectrums you believe define that mental state, in addition to those we just outlined.

Part three, emotion versus logic: if you do not fully understand parts one and two, go ahead and reread them, because it only gets more complicated. Every spectrum exists on both a logical plane and an emotional plane. They are both required. You can't ignore one of them. Even Aristotle knew this, with his theories of "logos" (logic) and "pathos" (emotion) as two-thirds of his rhetorical model. You must satisfy the logical spectrum, because while people make decisions based on emotional certainty, they only do so if they feel like they have logic's permission.

Let me explain: to persuade your audience to take an action, you must open the gate to their hearts. But to get

———

to that gate in the first place, you must open the gate to their logical minds, so that they feel safe giving way to their emotion. If asked, they'll say they took your suggested action because of their logical certainty. That's not true at all. Here's the truth: they took it because of their emotional certainty, and rationalized it with their logical certainty. No rationalization? No decision. That's why the logical spectrums are important; because they supply a logical rationalization that makes emotional decision-making feel more justifiable.

Part four, counterfactual simulation: this is an explanation of why the ideal mental state is so important. When your audience is considering taking your action, here's how they will decide: they will run a mental movie in their minds of how the future will probably look if they take your action. If that mental movie is positive, they will take your suggested action. If it is negative? They won't. What determines the nature of this mental movie? Their positions on the emotional and logical

———

quality spectrums that make up your ideal audience mindset.

## 1.25: MEANING THROUGH SEQUENCE

Compared to the last multi-part theory, this one is relatively simple. And it (like all these theories) explains structure theory. But (unlike all these theories) it does so in a particularly fundamental way.

Let's get into it. This theory of persuasive communication, quite simply, states that sequence matters, and that the order of your communication adds meaning to your communication.

Think about it. If we revisit the APP method, we see that the agree, *then* promise, *then* preview sequence is arranged that way because, due to that specific order and organization, it becomes more meaningful. Would the preview, promise, agree method work as well? Or the promise, preview, agree method? Or the preview, agree, promise? Probably not. We already talked about why APP in particular works. The agree phase establishes

———

---

empathy, gains trust, grabs attention, and highlights a problem. This foundation adds meaning and power to the promise phase, because promising a solution doesn't work as well if the person promising it is not empathetic, trusted, and doesn't have attention, or clearly brings up the problem the solution solves. It's like a step-ladder. Finally, the preview phase should come after the agree and promise phases because without the context of the promise, it doesn't make much sense at all. See how sequence matters?

So, remember this: structure theory yields specific, compelling, step-by-step language structures and communication patterns that build up meaning through their specific sequence of statements.

### 1.26: FRAMES

Much communication revolves around frames. Frames are relationships between things and actions that define the world. Frames often take the form of "X [verb] Y," or "X [verb clump]." For example: "climate-change is bad," (X verb Y), or "war should stop" (X verb clump). Sub-frames support top-level frames. "War should stop (X verb clump, top-level frame) because war is bad (X verb Y, supportive sub-frame one), because war is expensive (X verb Y, supportive sub-frame two), and because war is unnecessary (X verb Y, supportive sub-frame three)."

The structures you're going to learn are all designed to implicitly or explicitly reframe the world to your advantage. That's what you need to know about this theory.

That said, let's talk about one particularly elegant type of reframing: frame reversal, a type of frame escalation. In its simplest form, this means simply reversing an opposing frame. Not just countering with a new frame, but completely inverting the opposing frame and cancelling it out in totality. For example, if someone says that X contradicts Y, an elegant, persuasive, erudite, and compelling reframing is responding with, "actually, X does not only not contradict Y, but (new frame) X justifies Y." One particular structure uses reframing as its core foundation. You'll learn it soon.

### 1.27: UNSPOKEN WORDS

Here's the unfortunate truth: when you're attempting persuasive communication, you can't just come right out and say, "Trust me! I have empathy for you! Here's your problem, which is what I'm trying to sell you a solution to. I promise that this solution is worth-your-while! You should be curious about it. Be curious this instant!"

That sounds crazy. But there's no way around it: you want your audience to feel that way, don't you? Sure: you can't come right out and say those things. But you can use your three languages in such a way that your audience subconsciously receives that meaning; *that they hear those words subconsciously*; that they hear additional words that you have not actually said.

So, while you cannot come right out and say those things, you can use these structures, like the APP method, to convey unspoken words. In the case of the

APP method, the additional words are these: "Trust me! I have empathy for you (agree)! Here's your problem, which is what I'm trying to sell you a solution to. I promise that this solution is worth-your-while (promise)! You should be curious about it. Be curious this instant (preview)!"

Because you're implicitly communicating these words directly to your audience' subconscious minds, you can get away with it. In other words, you are embedding this meaning in the elegant face of the APP method. Get it? You wouldn't be able to come right out and just say those words, but you can impart them with this structure in an elegant and implicit but clear way.

So, to summarize, many of these structures and techniques are designed to communicate additional, unspoken words, which you would never be able to say out-loud, but which you must communicate somehow.

## 1.28: PERSUASIVE PATTERNS

We're so close. I can tell you want to get to structure theory, so I'll be quick. Combine the theories of additional words, frames, and meaning through sequence, and what do you get? You get the theory of persuasive patterns. What is this theory? That there are particular sequences of statements that establish the correct frames and make your audience hear specific additional unspoken words that work for any subject. In other words, there are specific language templates, which are persuasive patterns you can plug any specific nouns, verbs, and subjects into, and which work for all subjects. And, at long last…

## 1.29: STRUCTURE THEORY

These previous 28 theories characterize persuasive communication that works. Structure theory is summarized by this next sentence: *there are specific patterns of communication that satisfy the conditions of all of these theories, and that can be adapted to (almost) any subject and any speaker.*

---

Let's break this down. There are specific patterns of communication that...

Complete the public speaking triad as quickly as possible, with minimum effort and proven patterns you can instantly apply to any subject.

Maximize the power of your word language so that your words actually influence people and make them think and act the way you want them to, without coercion or cringy and forceful persuasion.

Activate new layers of your word language, and control it by aligning it with your purpose, so that your words don't go unnoticed and actually impact the people and world around you for the better.

Satisfy the ingredients for the persuasive public speaking triad to guarantee more successful persuasion without manipulative or forceful methods.

Move the world from starting-state to finishing-state and fulfill the purpose of your communication which gives you the insane power of being able to influence

---

———

reality with nothing but your words and some communication patterns.

Break down into structures for the beginning, middle, and end of your communication, so that the only simple, fast, and easy task remaining for you is to match a starting structure with a middle structure and an end structure.

Target subjects that bring you to the narrow top of the cone of attention and use language patterns that keep you there, which guarantees that people are going to be sitting on the edge of their seats listening to you, and that they are actually going to care about what you have to say.

Convey the right words in the right way, so that you don't embarrass yourself and fail at persuasive communication by bungling either the words or the way they're arranged, or both, and that you are guaranteed to at the very least be more compelling, if not 100-percent persuasive.

———

———

Appeal to self-interest and immediately answer the question "what's in it for me?" so that people will instantly respect you, instantly give you their undivided attention, and instantly take the actions you want them to take.

Convince your audience that marginal benefits far exceed marginal costs of paying you attention so that you can immediately balance the key persuasive equation and get people to act with a series of simple, easy, step-by-step language patterns.

Satisfy the mental checklist in the first eight seconds to guarantee that your audience sees you as someone with authority, as someone worth listening to, as someone who understands them, as someone who can help them get what they want, and as someone they are going to give undivided attention to for however long you ask for it.

Incorporate benefits and features so that your communication immediately highlights why your audience will benefit and how they will benefit, which *ceteris paribus*, guarantees, at the very least, immense interest, but more likely, easy persuasion.

Follow the moral of the wind and the sun and use gentle persuasion so that you don't have to barge into your audience's mental space, but instead can earn entry with gentle, subtle, professional persuasion that doesn't put anyone on edge or sacrifice your self-respect and image.

Create the proper mental state in your audience's mind so that they are willing, in fact enthusiastic, to do what you ask them to do, without you or them feeling like anyone got the better end of the deal.

Include only purpose statements and bridges, so that every single word you speak is important, meaningful, and powerful, which in turn grants you infinite respect in the eyes of your listeners who will not be able to help completely tuning in.

Target the right parts of the human-desire pyramid so that your audience instantly thinks to themselves "wow, I'm going to tune in and listen closely."

Accommodate audience uniqueness and audience personas to guarantee that you are saying the right things to the right people, and that you don't bungle important moments by saying the wrong things to the wrong people.

Focus on salient, intense, and stable subjects to instantly guarantee that you are speaking about the subjects that your audience wants to hear about, and that they will then give you the attention you need to persuade them.

Influence the outcome of your persuasion more than any other technique, and be the 20% of your communication that will make 80% of the difference in outcome, which you only need to be moderately competent with to instantly and easily improve your communication and its results.

Wield inherent elements of psychological persuasion to directly target the characteristics of human psychology that will give you unparalleled influence in communication.

————

Speak for action and use the proven principles of calling your audience to action to essentially guarantee that people do what you ask them to do, not feeling like they're doing you a favor, but feeling like they're taking action to help themselves.

Satisfy the 14Cs of communication so that your communication is worth listening to and so you don't blunder instead of actually communicating effectively.

Apply the principles of novelty and simplicity, which will instantly ensure that your audience is tuned in and enthusiastic about listening to you.

Produce emotional and logical certainty with counter-factual simulation and move your mental-state spectrums the way you want to move them, with a set of proven, reliable templates that are incredibly easy and straightforward to use.

Create meaning through sequence so that creating your communication is much easier and much more organized, which will make speech writing, presentation preparation, and any communication much faster to compose.

Produce compelling and persuasive frame effects that are designed to make your audience see things your way, which will make you an influential communicator.

Convey additional, implicit words to your audience which will bypass their conscious filters and punch straight to their subconscious minds, where real persuasion happens.

Incorporate persuasive patterns that are strategically designed to play upon human psychology for maximum persuasion, and that do not involve hard-sell aggressive persuasion tactics.

*Ceteris paribus*, make your life better, more fulfilling, and more rewarding, by giving you the one tool that makes the most difference at home, at work, and in your own mind: effective communication.

Now, I by no means claim to have all of the patterns and structures. In theory, there are thousands, if not an infinite number of them. But these 40-something structures are more than enough. And that's what I give you. I've looked, and I haven't found something like this anywhere else. I bought twenty books on this subject, and found nothing like this. I've read every article that might be related: nothing. I've bought courses and online training programs: nothing. You hold, in your lucky hands, the single key to the single theory of communication that will make the single important difference in your life by granting you the power of easy and effective persuasion and influence.

Where have I seen these patterns? Good question. I've used them myself, time and time again. I've seen my audiences *actually lean forward in their seats* as I would conclude one of these structures. When I was a competitive public speaker, competing in front of audiences of hundreds, I actually had people come up to me and say "when you start talking, I feel like time stops and I get carried into another world listening to you." That is a direct quote. And I've heard it, in different forms, more times than I can remember. Another

———

common occurrence for me, *specifically when I use these exact structures*, is this: I'm speaking in a loud, crowded room, whether it is a conference, competitive public speaking practice, or preliminary stages of a competition, and these structures work their magic. In other words: I'm there, practicing my speech, along with 20 to 30 other people. Then, I jump into one of these structures, and by the time I've finished it, everyone else has stopped their *own* practice, their *own* conversations, or whatever else they were doing across the room on their *own*, and immediately tuned in.

If my experience is not enough, I've also seen these structures used by business leaders, political leaders, and famous speakers. Remember, I first discovered structure theory listening to Bill Clinton. And then I confirmed what I saw in him in hundreds of other speeches.

My final words before getting right into it: this stuff is woven directly into almost all effective communication you hear, whether on purpose or by accident. Why not yours, and why not on purpose?

———

# CHAPTER TWO
# THE BASICS

---

## BUILDING OUT STRUCTURE THEORY

We'll begin getting into the speech structures now, with easy, step-by-step templates for each. Here's my promise: you are reading the most comprehensive guide to communication structure on the planet. This chapter is loaded with persuasive speech structures designed to instantly make persuading any audience much easier for you. And the best part? These are all proven structures, guaranteed to help your communication succeed. But before we get into the structures themselves, we must define some basic principles of effective structures.

## WHY THESE BASIC PRINCIPLES MATTER

Even professional public speakers get these wrong. Chances are you might too. And it gets worse. No matter how compelling your speech structure, if the basics aren't there, it is liable to fall apart. Some of these might be repetitive: that's intentional. They must be hammered into your mind. You can't forget them.

---

___

## THE CRUCIAL TRUTH ABOUT SPEECH STRUCTURE

It's simple: information is great. But if it's thrown at you in a random, disorganized sequence... well, it becomes useless. And you don't want to be useless when you are communicating, whether you are giving a public speech, speaking in a meeting, writing, selling, running for office, or, if you haven't gotten this by now, doing *any type of persuasive communication.*

Enter the solution: speech structure. Here's the crucial truth about speech structure: a brilliant speaker, speaking brilliant words, with brilliant vocal modulation and brilliant body language, will fail if the speech has no structure. Sad. A less experienced speaker, who is good but not great, will *easily* exceed the brilliant speaker if he has one thing: speech structure.

And sadly, most books, articles, or courses on this subject will give you three structures (that don't even apply to your situation), or variations of the "three-

___

point-punch" structure. But there's more to it than that. And I'll teach you everything.

## WHY SPEECH STRUCTURE IS SO IMPORTANT

Structure is so important because it organizes your information. Consider this: the same information placed in a different order can become less powerful or more powerful. In other words: the information doesn't change, but the sequence of the information does. It becomes structured, organized, and powerful.

Why do you want this? Because it makes your audience *love* listening to you. Because it makes people remember what you said. Because it helps you give a speech (or communicate through any medium) with more confidence. Because it helps you influence, motivate, persuade, or inform your audience.

## SIMPLICITY

I repeat: if you can say the same information in fewer words, do it. If you can use more simple, direct, and short words and sentences, do it. If you can structure your speech in a simpler way, do it.

## NOVELTY

I repeat: people crave new information. You *must* give a rapid-fire barrage of new information to your audience. Move from point to point quickly. This will keep them engaged and project your high value (as someone who has a lot of information and conveys it quickly).

## SIMPLICITY AND NOVELTY

Yes, they work together. You can provide rapid pieces of new information in a simple way.

## COGNITIVE LOAD

Too much information equals a high cognitive load, which equals a loss of attention. It's that simple. Don't overload your audience and increase their cognitive loads. Don't try to pack too much information in one chunk of communication. That said, another reason structure is so desirable in communication is because, by organizing your information according to one of these structures, you can increase the information per chunk of communication, but keep cognitive load down. Does this contradict novelty? Not necessarily. Novelty doesn't mean packing an excessive amount of information into your communication; it means conveying one idea fully, and then moving onto another instead of continuing to convey the first idea.

## ENGINEERED PERSUASION

The best persuasive communication is made persuasive not only by its content, but by its structure too. Two common methods of engineered persuasion (that are baked into the structure of the speech) are contrast persuasion and aspirational persuasion. In fact, contrast persuasion and aspirational persuasion often work together. We'll talk a lot more about how later on. It's incredibly powerful. For now, I'll just define the words (as they relate to speech structure).

Contrast persuasion refers to speech structures that use strategic contrasts between situations, solutions, or paths. These contrasts are incredibly persuasive.

Aspirational persuasion refers to speech structures that appeal to the aspirations of the audience. These aspirations drive people to action. I can't wait to show you speech structures that use both contrast and aspirational persuasion. You'll never look at communication the same way.

## TANGENTS OR PARANTHETICALS

A common mistake. Here's why these should be limited: they diminish the clarity of your message. They blur an otherwise clear, compelling, and commanding speech structure. They make you *appear* confused and make your audience *actually* confused (if they don't make you actually confused as well). One layer of tangents or parentheticals is okay, but not great. Two is not. Move in a logical, straight line from beginning to end.

## TRANSITIONS

You must use transitions to smooth the changes between parts of your speech. You must use transitions to provide context. These are the "bridges" we talked about. Why are transitions so powerful? Because they tell your audience information about the upcoming information. For example, if you say "on the contrary," it primes your audience to look for the differences between what you just said and what you're about to say. And that keeps them intellectually engaged with your speech. How do you determine your transitions? The simplest heuristic is to ask yourself this: "how does what I'm about to say relate to what I just said?"

## SIMILARITY OF STRUCTURE

All structures have three elements in common: the opening, the body, and the conclusion. The body usually takes up 80% of the allotted time, and also does 80% of the informing, persuading, inspiring, or entertaining. So, the body, because of that, will be the focus of this book.

## OPENINGS

Here's what openings have to accomplish: they must get attention in a way that is relevant to your message, they must act as a gateway into your content, they must set the expectations for the rest of your speech, and they must show the audience benefits of listening.

## COMMUNICATION BODY

This is where the magic happens. Here's speech structure defined in one sentence: changing the order of information in a speech to achieve desired effects on the audience. And almost all of that happens in the speech body. In other words, starting and closing speeches are completely different topics from structuring a speech. Structuring a speech has to do with the body of the speech. Opening a speech and closing a speech have to do with supporting the structure, although there are structures for doing these steps as well (although these are not covered in this book).

―――

## SPEECH CLOSINGS

Closings must include a call to action. After you've given your speech, if you've done it well, your audience will be thinking, "What do I do now?"

"How can I help?"

"What's the next step?"

And if you don't answer them, the entire speech is useless. You might as well have not given it.

Why? Because no real-world impact will happen. So please remember this: when you finish your speech, include a call to action.

―――

# CHAPTER THREE
# PERSUASIVE STRUCTURES

---

**MY PROMISE TO YOU**

This chapter will teach you exactly how to persuade your audience with speech structure. You'll learn proven, step-by-step persuasive structures like the "objection-prediction model." I promise that these persuasive speech structures will instantly make writing a persuasive speech easy, persuading an audience easy, and delivering a speech easy. Are you ready? Let's dive right into it.

**3.1: MONROE'S MOTIVATED SEQUENCE**
*What is it?*

A proven persuasive process that has worked since the 1930s. Five simple steps to persuading your audience.

*Why does it work?*

It forms a "yes-ladder" of positive persuasive momentum. It focuses on the problem before the proposed solution, so the solution makes more sense in context. It empowers the audience by focusing on their capacity for creating change through personal action.

---

___

### When do you use it?

When you want to persuade, motivate, or influence an audience. When you want to make a sales pitch. When you want to use a gentle, proven method of persuasion.

### What is the step-by-step process?

Attention: "Hey! Listen to me, you have a problem!" Need: "Let me explain the problem." Satisfaction: "But, I have a solution!" Visualization: "If we implement my solution, this is what will happen. Or, if we don't implement my solution, this is what will happen." Action: "You can help me, and you, in this specific way. Will you do it?"

This is one of my favorites. It has been studied, stress-tested, and proven to work. Additionally, it emphasizes three things: the problem, the solution, and the audience action. Here's why this is powerful: it makes your audience feel like they have power over the situation; like their personal actions can influence the outcomes. The result? They are more likely to act.

___

---

## 3.2: THE OBJECTION MODEL

### What is it?

Predicting the reasons your audience might object to your offer, then structuring your speech around addressing those objections.

### Why does it work?

It removes all the reasons your audience wouldn't accept your call to action. It clears the most common barriers to action. It leaves your audience no logical reason to not do what you ask of them.

### When do you use it?

When you have to persuade an audience. When you have to make a sales pitch. When you predict opposition to your proposal.

### What is the step-by-step process?

Discovery phase: discover the most common, probable objections to your proposal. Invalidation phase:

---

invalidate the objections. Construction phase: construct your speech around the reasons why those objections are invalid. Presentation phase: present a speech constructed around invalidating the objections you've discovered.

This one gets rid of all the reasons your audience won't do what you want. When you are persuading someone, you will be met with persuasion resistance. "Really…?" you ask, forlorn and dismayed. Yes. Almost always. Persuasion resistance often takes the form of specific objections to your offer, idea, or proposal. Here are some common examples: "I don't want to give anything up for it (which is a form of loss aversion: spending feels like a loss). I don't believe it can work. I don't think it can work for me. I can wait. I think it's too difficult. I don't understand it. I don't understand why I need it. I don't believe it will do what is promised. I don't know if it fits into my life. I don't trust the speaker."

And with this speech structure, you quickly remove all the audience objections.

———

Here are some bonus guidelines: counter each objection at the exact moment your audience might be thinking it. Counter the right objections: don't counter objections that people don't have. If you are a trustworthy authority, then trusting you isn't a common objection. In this case, don't talk about your credentials over and over. You would be countering an objection that doesn't exist. Do not directly say the objections. Only say your counters. Don't say, "Now you might be thinking it costs too much... but it's $3,000 less than our competitors." Instead, just say "It's $3,000 less than our competitors." Why? Saying the objection puts it in their heads if they weren't thinking about it. (In the spirit of full honesty, there is some dispute on this point. This is just the conclusion of my intuition).

This structure is four steps. What do they do? They remove all barriers your audience has to accepting your offer (assuming you do it right). Easy, simple, and straightforward.

———

___

### 3.3: PATH CONTRAST

#### What is it?

Structuring your speech by contrasting two different possible paths. Contrasting a "good" proposed path with a "bad" alternative.

#### Why does it work?

It frames the contrast between the two paths, which allows you to control the narrative. It uses contrast persuasion, one of the most effective persuasive methods. It makes your proposed path seem like the obvious choice.

#### When do you use it?

When you want to persuade, motivate, or inspire your audience to take one path instead of another. When there is uncertainty about how to proceed. When the future is unclear and you want to lead the way.

___

---

### *What is the step-by-step process?*

Good path: "Here's the good path we should take."
Good outcome: "Here are the good things that will
happen if we do." Alternative path: "Or, here's a bad
alternative path we could take." Alternative outcome:
"And here are the bad outcomes that will happen if we
do." Back-and-forth: jump back and forth between
describing the good path and the alternative path.

Let me tell you a secret: persuasion is more powerful
when it has contrast. In other words, if you want people
to take a path, don't only talk about the benefits of that
path. Contrast the "good" path with an alternative "bad"
path.

So, don't only say this: "Imagine our lives when we
take [good path]. We will [insert benefit one], [insert
benefit two], and [insert benefit three]."

You must also say this: "Imagine our lives when we
take [bad path]. We will [insert consequence one], [insert
consequence two], and [insert consequence three]."

---

And then jump back and forth between them. Hit the contrast button over and over again. Make it a glaring, obvious, clear answer that they should take the good path. How? By repeatedly and vividly contrasting it with a bad one.

Why is this such a powerful strategy? The contrast between the "good" and "bad" outcome is more persuasive than either of them alone. Presenting a "good" option that you want, and a "bad" alternative, makes doing what you want the obvious action. I repeat: making it seem like a contrast between two options allows you to control the narrative.

## 3.4: PAST, PRESENT, MEANS
### *What is it?*
Presenting the problems of a difficult past, shifting to the easy, successful present, and explaining how you (or the "main character" of this story) made the transition.

### Why does it work?

It builds audience relatability by resonating emotionally. It shows the contrast between having unsolved problems and solved problems. It makes the "means" extremely desirable and builds immense suspnese.

### When do you use it?

When you want to influence or persuade your audience to do something (whatever your "means" are). When your proposed action worked personally for you in your life, or you have a compelling and clear case-study. When your life before taking the proposed action matches the lives of your audience now.

### What is the step-by-step process?

Past: "Here's how my life was difficult in the past. Here were my unsolved problems. I was suffering in the ways you are suffering." Present: "Here's how my life is successful now. Here's what it's like to have the problems solved. Here's how I'm no longer suffering,

———

and life is easy." Means: "Here's the exact solution I personally used to get from the difficult past to the successful present."

This speech structure is so powerful. The entire time you're in the past and present stages, your audience is going *crazy,* wondering: "How did you do it? How did you solve the problem? Help me! Can you please show me the solution? I need this in my life! I want to do what you did!"

And then you hit them with that solution. At this point, there's almost nothing that can stop them from taking it (whether it's something they buy, or something they simply do).

The curiosity, suspense, and intrigue built up during the two phases of your personal story (past and present) are too strong.

Here are the crucial principles. Humility: yes, you solved the problem they are struggling with. Yes, you still have to be humble about it.

———

Honesty: don't make your past and present seem like anything other than what they are.

Relatability: is your past really similar to the current lives of your audience members? Can they read themselves into you story (or the story of your "main character?")

Emotional resonance: can you accurately depict the emotions you felt during the difficult past? Can you convey them to your audience? If you do, will they think "wow, that's exactly how I feel right now?"

And here are some important guidelines: don't present the solution until step three. In other words, don't let step two and three blend. In step two, only explain the relief from the problem. Don't explain how it happened. This builds curiosity and suspense. Show vulnerability in step one: be open, honest, and willing to expose parts of your past. In step three, describe the solution at length. Emphasize how it worked for you. Imply that if it worked for you, it can work for them, or flat-out state this.

### 3.5: PROBLEM-SOLUTION FORMULA

**What is it?**

Presenting a clear problem your audience has, and then presenting a solution to that problem.

**Why does it work?**

It ensures that your audience understands why your solution matters. It educates your audience and provides value. It points out a problem which your audience might not have known about.

**When do you use it?**

When you want to persuade your audience to solve a problem. When they might not be aware of the problem, or how serious it is. When you are selling a solution.

**What is the step-by-step process?**

Problem presentation: "Here's a problem you face." Problem consequences: "Here's why this problem is worse than you think." Solution presentation: "But there's a solution." Solution outcome: "Here's what it will feel like when you solve the problem."

This persuasive speech structure is so simple but so powerful. Why? Because most people make the mistake of only talking about their solution, which is weaker, because a solution only makes sense in the context of a problem. In other words: why do so many people talk about their solutions without first explaining the problem it solves? Because they haven't read this book. But you have :) Time for number six: a structure very similar to this one.

## 3.6: DIAGNOSE, PROBLEM, SOLUTION
### *What is it?*
Diagnosing a problem which people know they have but not why they have it, then providing a solution.

___

### Why does it work?

It implies you know how to solve the problem you diagnosed. It uses contrast persuasion (problem versus solution). It gives you authority as the "diagnoser."

### When do you use it?

When you want to persuade your audience to solve a problem. When they are aware of the problem, but don't understand it. When you know why a problem exists, but your audience doesn't.

### What is the step-by-step process?

Diagnose: "You already know you have this problem. But here's exactly WHY you have this problem. Here's what causes it." Problem: "Here's why this problem is worse than you think." Solution: "Now that I've diagnosed this problem, let me tell you how to solve it."

If you're wondering how this is different from the problem-solution structure, here's how: the problem-solution structure is for audiences who aren't fully aware

___

―――

of a problem. The diagnose-problem-solution structure is for audiences who are aware of a problem, but not why it exists.

Why diagnose the problem at all? Because it builds trust and presents your authority. The audience thinks that the person who understands why a problem exists is the one best equipped to fix it. They're probably right, by the way. And the person who is best equipped to fix a problem is probably the best person to buy a solution to that problem from. Get it?

And another captivating rhetorical structure is this: the diagnose phase can consist of not only properly diagnosing what the problem *is*, but telling the audience what it is *not*. "The problem is not [insert superficial problem one], it is not [insert superficial problem two], it is not [insert superficial problem three], [repeat as many as you want]. The problem is [insert deep problem that causes the previous superficial problems; the underlying disease that causes the symptoms that are those superficial problems]."

―――

___

## 3.7: CRITERIA MATCHING

### *What is it?*

Presenting the criteria which define the best option, and then proving that your proposal meets them.

### *Why does it work?*

It focuses on establishing agreement first. It builds speaker to audience rapport. It builds a two-step "yes-ladder" by first agreeing on what criteria matter and only then presenting an option.

### *When do you use it?*

When you want to persuade your audience to choose your option out of many options. When there are generally agreed-upon criteria for judging what makes this type of thing the best, or when it is easy to establish such criteria.

___

### *What is the step-by-step process?*

Criteria establishment: "Here's what makes this type of thing good. Can we agree on that? We agree, so far, on what this type of thing would need to be good, right?" Criteria satisfaction: "As you can see, my proposed option fills the criteria we just agreed on."

Like many of these persuasive speech structures, this one is a yes-ladder. Here's what that means: instead of getting right into the hard-sell, it slowly builds up to it. Along the way, it gets a series of "yes" responses.

"Yes, those are definitely the criteria I'm looking to fill for this type of solution."

"Yes, that checklist seems reasonable."

"Yes, I guess your option does fill the checklist." "

"Yes, that means your option fills the criteria."

"Yes, that means your option is the best."

"Yes, since it is the best, I should buy it or agree with your point of view."

Due to the principle of persuasive consistency (people want to be consistent with their previous actions), here's what happens: with every additional "yes," the chances of hearing a "no" decrease. In other words, you gain "yes-momentum." Compare that to jumping straight to it: "No, I don't think your option is the best. What are the criteria you're using to judge that? I bet you have none. No, since it's not the best, I won't take it. Go away."

## 3.8: CRITERIA MATCHING, DEMATCHING
### *What is it?*
Presenting the criteria which define the best option. Proving that all other options don't meet them (criteria de-matching). Proving that your option does (criteria matching).

### *Why does it work?*
It has all the benefits of criteria matching. It adds another persuasive layer to the equation. It turns "mine is good," to "mine is good, the others aren't." It makes

your audience think twice about considering another option.

### When do you use it?

When criteria matching fits. When there are multiple options in fierce competition. When you aren't concerned about discrediting an opponent's position.

### What is the step-by-step process?

Criteria establishment: "Here's what makes this type of thing good. Can we agree on that? We agree, so far, on what this type of thing would need to be good, right?" Criteria satisfaction: "As you can see, my proposed option fills the criteria we just agreed on." Criteria dissatisfaction: "As you can see, the other options clearly don't fit the checklist. Thus, the other options aren't the best."

___

### 3.9: THE SIX-POINT PUNCH

***What is it?***

A quick, assertive, hard-sell approach for fast sales pitches (even if you're selling an idea).

***Why does it work?***

It is designed to pack the most persuasion into the smallest amount of time. It is designed to convince people as quickly as possible. It is brief, but psychologically persuasive.

***When do you use it?***

When you don't have a lot of time. When you aren't trying to pitch a big commitment. When you are trying to persuade an audience to buy (instead of another action), although it does work for adopting ideas as well.

***What is the step-by-step process?***

Unique value proposition and headline statement: "Here's why this product offers unique value to you.

Here's why you should pay attention." Supporting statement: "Normally, this type of product causes [insert pain point or inconvenience]. But this model offers [repeat unique value] without [insert pain point or inconvenience]." Physical description (if applicable): "Here's what it looks like. Here's what it feels like." Benefit statements: "It will [insert benefit one], [insert benefit two], [insert benefit three]." Call-to-action: "Do this to get it." Trust indicators and social proof: "These people bought it too, and here's what they have to say about it."

Humans have a central processing route and a peripheral processing route. The peripheral route controls are mental processes dictating impulsive, emotional decisions, and the central route controls mental processes dictating big commitments. The central route is careful, slow, and logical.

The six-point-punch targets the peripheral route. This next structure is for selling people on big commitments, targeting the central route.

___

### 3.10: ECONOMIC VALUES STRUCTURE

**What is it?**

Presenting a product, and then showing how it satisfies the nine economic values.

**Why does it work?**

It is designed to give potential customers as much information as possible. It is designed to convince people to make big commitments. It is designed to make your audience trust you.

**When do you use it?**

When you are selling a complex, expensive product. When you are trying to get people to make a big financial commitment. When you are selling via the central processing route.

**What is the step-by-step process?**

Product presentation: "Here's what it is, what it does, and how it does it." Efficacy: "Here's how well it does

___

what it's supposed to do. Speed: "Here's how quickly you'll get results." Reliability: "Here's how reliable it is." Ease of Use: "Here's how easy it is to use." Flexibility: "Here's how many things it can do." Status: "Here's how it will make others see you." Aesthetic Appeal: "Here's how aesthetically pleasing it is." Emotion: "Here's how it makes you feel." Cost: "Here's how much it costs."

This speech structure is perfect for selling big, expensive things. Why? Because it builds trust. Because it is education-based selling (teaching about a product rather than trying to sell it from the start). Because it speaks in terms of the economic values people use to evaluate products.

And if you're thinking "it seems a little too long," guess what? You can leave out certain economic values. You can reorder them to put the important ones first. But the truth is this: persuasion via the central route demands deliberate information-exchange and time-commitment. No shortcuts.

---

### 3.11: SHORT-FORM RHETORICAL THREE-POINT PUNCH

**What is it?**

Structuring a speech by making a claim, and supporting that claim with an emotional subpoint, an evidence-driven subpoint, and a logical subpoint.

**Why does it work?**

Because it uses the three proven rhetorical methods (evidence, logic, and emotion). Because it is memorable. Because it is flexible.

**When do you use it?**

When you want to give a brief persuasive speech. When you want to change someone's point-of-view. When you are persuading, but not selling.

**What is the step-by-step process?**

Main claim: "X should Y because [emotional reason], [logical reason], and [evidence-driven reason].

---

———

Emotional reason: "X should Y because it hurts people. Here's how…" Logical reason: "X should Y because it is inherently self-contradictory. Here's how…" Evidence-driven reason: "X should Y because 9/10 doctors say so. Here's why…"

Let me explain why this is so powerful. Centuries ago, Aristotle boiled down all of persuasion to three things: emotion (pathos), logic (logos), and evidence (ethos), which includes evidence creating the perception that the speaker is trustworthy and has the best interests of the audience at heart. And with this structure, you're using each of them to support a main claim.

If you have to give a brief persuasive speech, just answer these questions: What do I want to persuade people of? What's an emotional reason they should agree with me? What's a logical reason they should agree with me? What's the evidence that should make them agree with me?

And once you do that, you have your brief persuasive speech! But let's say you want to give a longer persuasive

———

speech using these principles. For that, we have this next structure. Like an accordion, it stretches out the short-form three-point-punch. (A quick side note: lengthening, shortening, and structure-stacking are huge. We'll talk about them later. Keep them filed in the back of your mind).

### 3.12: LONG-FORM RHETORICAL THREE-POINT PUNCH

*What is it?*

Structuring a speech by making one claim, and supporting that claim with three sub-points, each of which have ethos, pathos, and logos within them.

*Why does it work?*

It extends the short-form rhetorical three-point-punch. It is more substantial. It uses three times as much emotion, three times as much logic, and three times as much evidence as the short-form version.

―――

### When do you use it?

When you want to give a longer persuasive speech. When you want to change someone's point-of-view, but they are *particularly* entrenched. When you need extra persuasive power.

### What is the step-by-step process?

Main claim: "X should Y because [reason one], [reason two], and [reason three]. Reason one: "[Reason one] [emotional details], [logical details], [evidence]." Reason two: "[Reason two] [emotional details], [logical details], [evidence]." Reason three: "[Reason three] [emotional details], [logical details], [evidence]."

I know exactly what you're thinking: "what's the difference between this and the last one?" The short-form version is essentially just one third of the long-form version. The long-form version is basically three of the short-form versions stacked together, in support of one broader claim.

―――

Now, let's move away from the three-point, six-point, and extended-three-point punches. Enough punches. Time for a series of persuasive *trifectas*. These are some of my favorite structures. They are easy, simple, and powerful. You'll see once you use them for yourself. They are uniquely effective at changing minds and influencing people.

### 3.13: GAIN, LOGIC, FEAR TRIFECTA
*What is it?*
Structuring a persuasive speech around an audience gain, logical justifications of the gain, and then fear of missing the gain.

*Why does it work?*
It uses tantalizing benefits to get audience attention. It plays on the "fear of missing out." It combines gain and fear with logic, to make the whole structure appeal properly to reason instead of just emotion.

---

### When do you use it?

When you want to persuade the audience to do something that will help them. When the thing that the audience gains from also helps you. When your offer expires soon, or there is a time limit, or there is some scarcity involved, like limited resources.

### What is the step-by-step process?

Present subject: "Here's what I want you to do." Create gain: "Here are all the benefits you'll gain from doing it. Aren't they great?" Justify with logic: "Here's the logical proof of the gain." Instill fear: "But act fast! The offer expires in 24 hours. Then, you won't be able to gain anything!"

*Fear.* It is so incredibly, unbelievably, *extremely* powerful. People have risen to positions of world leadership with fear persuasion *and almost nothing else.*

The gain-logic-fear trifecta can convince almost anyone of anything. It is so powerful because of that final step, when you make people fear missing out. Why?

―――

Because of loss aversion: people hate losing things, and generally anticipate the pain of loss to feel twice as intense as the pleasure of gain.

And when you use this structure, here's what your audience will be thinking: "I would hate to figure out later that I really needed this. I don't want to miss this opportunity to take action now. I'm afraid I'll pass the offer, and then regret it."

### 3.14: TENSION, DESIRE, ACTION TRIFECTA
*What is it?*
Structuring a persuasive speech around creating tension in the audience's minds, building desire through tension, and then providing an action by which to escape tension.

*Why does it work?*
It uses cognitive dissonance in the audience to get action. It uses aspirational persuasion. It captures attention through tension.

―――

---

## When do you use it?

When your audience has a clear unfulfilled area of improvement. When your audience isn't living in the best way or fulfilling their fullest potential. When you have a solution for the previous two problems.

## What is the step-by-step process?

Create tension: "You aren't living your best life. Here's what you want to be: [insert aspirations]. Do your actions line up with who you want to be? No. You could be better." Build desire: "Imagine what it would feel like to finally be on the path you want to be on. Imagine how relaxed you would feel, knowing that you are acting in alignment with your desires and values." Propose action: "Here's a way you can be on that path."

Here's what this structure is basically doing: creating cognitive dissonance, or "the state of having inconsistent thoughts, beliefs, or attitudes, especially as relating to behavioral decisions and attitude change."

---

In other words, you're pointing out the gaping gaps between who your audience members want to be, or even think they already are, and who they *actually* are.

At this point, because of the tension created by the cognitive dissonance, the desire is huge. They crave a way to close the gap you just pointed out between "who I want to be or who I think I already am" and "who I actually am." They probably want an easy, quick, simple way to close the gap. And that's exactly what you'll give them in the action step.

### 3.15: PERSUASIVE STACK STRUCTURE
*What is it?*

Structuring a persuasive speech around Dr. Robert Cialdini's six proven principles of psychological persuasion outlined in his book *Influence: The Psychology of Persuasion.*

_____

### *Why does it work?*

It uses proven, scientific methods of persuasion. It uses all six of the persuasive principles in sequence. It is flexible.

### *When do you use it?*

When you want to make your audience like you. When you want to use a gentle, subtle form of persuasion. When you want to give a conversational speech.

### *What is the step-by-step process?*

Use likeability: "I am trying to [insert common goal with your audience]. You guys are [insert compliment]. I also [insert similarity]." Use reciprocity: "Normally I don't do this, but here's this free report that covers more than I can cover in this speech. People usually pay $200 for it, but it's free for you guys." Use authority: "Here's why I'm an expert on this subject. Here's why you should trust me. Here are my credentials." Use consensus: "Not a lot of people used to agree with me. Now, 86% of

_____

people do." Use scarcity: "But time is running out. We have to take action fast, or else we won't be able to." Use consistency: "Do you all agree with [small claim]? What about [slightly larger claim]? Maybe also [medium claim]? Do you also agree with [large, primary claim]?"

Let's break it down a little: people like those who have common goals as them, who compliment them, and who are similar to them. And if your audience likes you, they are more likely to accept your persuasion.

You are more likely to persuade your audience if you give them something. Why? They feel the need to reciprocate that action.

You are more likely to persuade people if they see you as an authority. This is also psychologically programmed.

People follow those around them. They look to others to decide how to act. So, when you tell them that "86% of people believe this," they are more likely to believe it too. This is consensus.

―――

We talked about scarcity already. Remember? It is the "fear of missing out" in the Tension-Desire-Action structure.

Last but not least: if you get people to agree to smaller claims, that "yes momentum" will carry over to larger claims. This is part of a "yes-ladder." Why? People want to be consistent with their actions. Now, I have a whole section from my previous book (*How to Master Public Speaking*) on this subject. I'll give it to you for free, because this is really important. Here it is: "There are six basics of persuasion. While this is not necessarily a direct aspect of public speaking, injecting these into your speech, leading up to it, or even after it when interacting with audience members, will make you very persuasive. These are all scientifically backed and have been proven to work time and time again. Know them, and use them. You'll see how effective they are for yourself.

Reciprocity: people tend to feel the need to repay any kind behavior they receive. If a friend buys you lunch, there's an obligation to buy them lunch in the future to return the favor. If you give another speaker a standing ovation, they are likely to reciprocate this behavior back to you later on. If you want to persuade the audience to buy a product from you, giving them a discount on it will make them more likely to buy it because you are essentially giving up money you would have earned for them to give up money in return.

Interestingly enough, how you give the discount is just as important as the discount itself. If you say "there's a 10% discount on my product," that may only attract a few buyers from the audience. However, if you say "now I normally only offer a 5% discount on my product at the end of these speeches, but because you were such a great audience, I'll give a 10% discount. Make sure you don't tell anyone!" the results will be much more profitable. You are giving the same discount in both cases, but in one situation you are doing it in a much more personal way. Additionally, by including the "don't tell anyone!" you are entering into a lighthearted, friendly conspiracy with the audience.

To appear more genuine, you can even announce the 5% discount, leave the microphone, but then turn back and say "actually, I think such a great audience deserves a 10% discount." By exchanging this kindness with the audience, they are much more likely to buy the product because they will be supporting someone they like. People will never admit the reason they bought it is because they like you; they will form a logical rationalization to use as an explanation of their purchase. If you recall, most decisions are made on emotion, not logic, and yet most decisions are consciously rationalized by logic after they are made on an emotional impulse.

Scarcity: people want things that other people don't have. That is why people buy expensive jewels. They serve no real function, but are desirable because of their rarity. An example of scarcity in action is when a consumer product in the market decreases in availability, and the prices go up. The product itself is the same, but because there is less of it available on the market, people are willing to pay more for it.

The underlying subconscious assumption behind this behavioral phenomenon is that a rare resource will run out faster, and that more people are competing for the same resource.

You can use the principle of persuasive scarcity in a speech by portraying your idea or product as one your audience should adopt soon, because if they do not, they will soon regret losing the opportunity as it will be sold out or too late. Loss aversion is a very powerful motivator: people typically don't play to win, just not to lose. Losing out on the opportunity to buy or do something, even if one hasn't already, triggers loss aversion as well.

Many online stores use scarcity to spur purchases, which is a highly effective strategy. They do so by putting a timed discount, or a decreasing stock number. Just as scarcity can work on an online store, it can work in your speech. Don't create fake scarcity: if fake scarcity is detected by your audience, which it likely will be, then they will feel manipulated or lied to. If there is even a small amount of scarcity, then expose it. Don't make it up, just express it if it already exists.

Authority: ethos and the persuasive principle of authority are very similar. They are using what people of authority on a subject have said about it to help validate your point. The principle of personal authority is when you try to generate the appearance of being an authority on a subject, and thereby ethos is automatically generated whenever you say something. You can create this appearance by explaining complex aspects of an idea, problem, or product to your audience. Additionally, you can briefly mention the amount of research that supports what you are saying, or briefly allude to your credentials. Anything that makes you appear as an expert on a subject generates personal ethos. Personal ethos is a very powerful tool for persuading an audience. Harnessing this principle of persuasion can go a long way; you are making use of the reason why patients defer to the judgements of doctors, and athletes listen to their coaches.

An interesting example of the principle of authority is the Milgram experiment, which showed that people would willingly shock what they believed to be a real person in another room at higher and higher voltages, and even at lethal voltages. They did so because an authority figure told them to. Nobody was actually shocked; the test participant was just made to believe that someone was being shocked. Why did they do this? Why did they willingly shock another human being, despite having clear reservations about it? Because an authority figure told them to.

Determining what people are willing to do just because an authority figure told them to was the purpose of the famous Milgram experiment, and it found that authority is an incredibly powerful quality. Just make sure you use it for good.

Consistency: people want to be consistent with themselves. The principle of persuasive consistency suggests that it is easier to get someone to agree to

---

something substantial if you've gotten them to agree to something smaller in the past.

If you approach someone and ask them directly for a donation to a nonprofit, they will likely say no, but if you approach someone and first ask them to verbally endorse a nonprofit, and then ask for a donation later on, they are much more likely to say yes to making the donation if they previously agreed to a verbal endorsement.

People like to be consistent with themselves. If you've gotten someone to agree to something small, they are more likely to agree to something bigger later on. If you try to get someone to agree to something big immediately, they are far more likely to turn you down than if you ease them into it by first getting them to make smaller commitments. Doing so is essentially forming a "ladder" in which each rung of the ladder represents a slightly larger commitment than the last. Whether the commitment is to purchase something or to agree with someone, the principle of consistency applies. If your

———

audience agrees first to a small claim you make, and then to a slightly more controversial claim, and then to your most contentious point, you are more likely to get them to agree to your most contentious point than if you started with it.

Likability: the fable of the Wind and the Sun is instructive here. There is a lot to learn from this fable. In some cases, it is better to be gentle when persuading. Some people grow defensive when faced with aggressive persuasion tactics, and instead of getting anything out of them, they tighten their metaphorical coats. The sun gently shined its warmth on the traveler, and the traveler took off the coat on his own.

In many cases, subtle and gentle persuasion beats obvious persuasion. The coat represents an inherent aversion to be persuaded that many carry like a shield. Indeed, persuasion resistance is a well-documented psychological phenomenon. Many assume that if you try to persuade them of something, it must be beneficial for you at their expense. Do not try to rip the shield from

———

people for that will surely fail. On the other hand, get them to willingly give up their shield just as the traveler took off his coat.

The principle of likeability embodies the moral of Aesop's fable. People prefer to help those who they like. People tend to like those who are similar to them, have complimented them, or who are working towards similar goals as them. Employ these to get people to like you before trying to persuade them to your cause.

It is well known that in business, if you want to convince someone to make a big purchase or commitment, you don't want to get right to business. Take them to a business dinner, ask about their day, exchange pleasantries, see how their family is doing, and ignore the business for the first half hour or so. During this time set aside the business and focus on establishing similarity, complimenting them, and looking for common goals. Only after establishing a bond of friendship with the prospective buyer is it time to bring up business.

———

At this point, because they view you as a friend, they will subconsciously not want to turn you down in fear that they might lose the connection. Humans are inherently social creatures, and we are genetically predisposed to value a large social network. Many businessmen say that it is better to "get right into it," but it has been proven time and time again that the approach of fostering likeability for a few minutes and then getting into the business is much more effective and results in more profitable agreements for both parties.

Use the principle of likability often in your speech. It can often make the difference between people following your call to action or ignoring it. You can use the principle of likability in your speech by establishing common goals with your audience, expressing similarity, and complimenting them. Specifically how to do this will be answered in the Audience Interaction section.

A last word on the principle of likability and soft persuasion is this: you cannot force anyone to listen to your speech. They may be sitting there, but it is up to

———

you to persuade them to listen. Just because you have an audience doesn't mean your audience is listening. How do you make them listen? By making them *choose* to listen. They cannot be forced. This evokes the same truth as the fable of the wind and the sun. Be so valuable as a speaker, with such important ideas and such an engaging presence, that they almost *have* to choose to listen.

Consensus: the herd mindset is an interesting phenomenon. A study conducted by researchers at Leeds University concluded that ten confident people who pretended to know what they were doing in an unfamiliar situation were able to influence 190 people to follow them. The principle of consensus plays off of the tendency people have to follow the crowd, or a few particularly confident people from the crowd. This principle applies especially in times of uncertainty. You can use this principle to your advantage by asking a group of friends who you know will be attending your speech to give a standing ovation after you finish. Upon

———

seeing five or six people stand, others will begin to follow their lead. This is simply how human beings are wired. Here's how a speaker attempting to persuade an audience could use the previous six persuasive principles: "Hey everyone. How are you all? It's nice to be in Boston. I'm from New York, but the Patriots are still my favorite football team. I used to live here. This is a great city full of great people. I think the best part of Boston culture that I brought to New York with me is to try to do the best I possibly can in everything. Today, my goal is to help you all do the best you possibly can when it comes to saving our planet and saving money. Now there are a lot of ways we can do this. In fact, there are too many for me to possibly go over. So, before I begin, if you want to write your emails on that clipboard that's being passed around, I'll share my 100-page report on how you can be more climate friendly and save lots of your money at the same time. At my last speech I charged them for it, but I'll give it to you all for free since we're in my hometown. Now, let's get into it. I graduated

———

from Harvard University and immediately entered the field of climatology, and worked as a climatologist with the government for 14 years. I've been responsible for many breakthroughs, I've filmed a few documentaries, and I've even been lucky enough to travel the world to meet with other scientists. I don't know too much about a lot of things, but I do know a lot about one thing: climate change. Luckily for us, that's true for a lot of people nowadays. When I started working as a climatologist, three out of every ten people believed in climate change. Now, eight out of every ten people do. When I started, one out of every ten people actively tried to live climate friendly lives. Now, seven out of every ten do. To me, it's wonderful that the vast majority of people are beginning to become more aware about the environment. Here's an important point to take note of, though: awareness is great and all, but if we want to make a real difference, if we want to prevent floods in our hometowns, if we want to prevent famine and drought, we really do need to start making change now. Time is

———

running out. I'll get back to this point later, but now let me ask you some questions. You can just answer these in your heads. First, do you agree that as humans, we do have an effect on our environment, even if it's not a bad one? Do you agree that just by our activities we change the environment from its natural state? I think it's safe to say that yes, we do. Now, let me ask you this: do you agree that some of the effects we have on our environment can be good? I think it's reasonable to say that yes, some of them can be. What about this: do you agree that some of them are bad? Probably yes, right? Now last question: do you agree that the bad effects outweigh the good, and the consequences need to be prevented by active effort on all our parts?"

Hopefully you were able to pick out the instances of each of the persuasive methods. The speaker used all six. Here's how:

"Hey everyone. How are you all? It's nice to be in Boston. I'm from New York, but the Patriots are still my favorite football team. I used to live here. This is a great city full of great people. I think the best part of Boston culture that I brought to New York with me is to try to do the best I possibly can in everything. Today, my goal is to help you all do the best you possibly can when it comes to saving our planet and saving money. *[The first principle of persuasion used in this speech is likability. Up until this point, the climatologist fostered likeability by establishing similarity to his audience (the Patriots are still my favorite football team), by complimenting his audience in a way that seems genuine (this is a great city full of great people), and by establishing common goals (my goal is to help you all do the best you possibly can when it comes to saving our planet and saving money).]* Now there are a lot of ways we can do this. In fact, there are too many for me to possibly go over. So, before I begin, if you want to write your emails on that clipboard that's being passed around, I'll share my 100-page report on how you can be more climate friendly and save lots of your money at the same time. At my last speech I charged them for it, but I'll give it to you all for free since we're in my hometown. *[The second principle of persuasion used in this*

―――

*speech is reciprocity. Immediately, the climatologist begins by offering an immensely valuable gift to his audience. Now, they feel that they need to repay the favor. Perhaps they won't gift a physical object to the speaker, but instead they will gift their attention and respect to him. Note that he didn't make the offering in the format of "here's [gift]- actually, here's [bigger gift] for you nice people. Instead, he made the offering in the format of "here's [gift] because of [reason]." Both are effective, seem genuine, and generate reciprocity. Another possibility is "here's [gift]- actually, here's [bigger gift] because of [reason]. Regardless, they all serve to effectively build reciprocity.]* Now, let's get into it. I graduated from Harvard University and immediately entered the field of climatology, and worked as a climatologist with the government for 14 years. I've been responsible for many breakthroughs, I've filmed a few documentaries, and I've even been lucky enough to travel the world to meet with other scientists. I don't know too much about a lot of things, but I do know a lot about one thing: climate change. *[The third principle of persuasion used in this speech is authority. The speaker establishes authority when he says*

―――

*he graduated from Harvard, immediately became a climatologist, worked with the government for 14 years and accomplished breakthroughs, worked on documentaries, and traveled the world to meet other scientists. One important note is this: while he did explain his credentials and in doing so built authority, he also interjected humble comments. This occurred when he said "I've even been lucky enough," and "I don't know too much about a lot of things." It's important to express humility and gratitude when trying to express authority.]* Luckily for us, that's true for a lot of people nowadays. When I started working as a climatologist, three out of every ten people believed in climate change. Now, eight out of every ten people do. When I started, one out of every ten people actively tried to live climate friendly lives. Now, seven out of every ten do. To me, it's wonderful that the vast majority of people are beginning to become more aware about the environment. *[The fourth principle of persuasion used in this speech is consensus. The speaker accomplished this by stating the previous statistics which clearly indicate that the vast majority of people now believe in climate change.]* Here's an important

———

point to take note of, though: awareness is great and all, but if we want to make a real difference, if we want to prevent floods in our hometowns, if we want to prevent famine and drought, we really do need to start making change now. Time is running out. *[The fifth principle of persuasion used in this speech is scarcity. The speaker accomplished this by stating that there is a limited, rapidly closing window for action. Scarcity can be created in either of these forms: "we must do [action] before the little time remaining runs out," or "we must do [action] before the necessary resources run out." These are similar, and indeed, time is a resource. Both become more powerful if a specific number is attached to the scarcity, such as a small number of years, for example.]* I'll get back to this point later, but now let me ask you some questions. You can just answer these in your heads. First, do you agree that as humans, we do have an effect on our environment, even if it's not a bad one? Do you agree that just by our activities we change the environment from its natural state? I think it's safe to say that yes, we do. Now, let me ask you this: do you agree that some of the effects we have on our

———

environment can be good? I think it's reasonable to say that yes, some of them can be. What about this: do you agree that some of them are bad? Probably yes, right? Now last question: do you agree that the bad effects outweigh the good, and the consequences need to be prevented by active effort on all our parts? *[Lastly, the sixth and final principle of persuasion used by the speaker is consistency. This was a classic "yes ladder." The speaker began by asking the audience if they agree to a very agreeable claim. Then, a slightly less agreeable claim. Then another agreeable claim. Then another less agreeable claim, followed by the main claim that the climatologist wants his audience to agree with. At this point, the speaker had created the positive "yes momentum" of four preceding agreements before actually asking the main question. A less experienced speaker would have skipped those.]*"

Do you see the effect created by those principles being used together? By the end of the speech, the audience was probably thinking "wow, what a reasonable guy. I definitely agree with him. I'm going to

———

read his report tonight and start doing some of the steps."

### 3.16: LAST METHOD
### *What is it?*

Structuring a persuasive speech around discrediting all other methods, and then presenting one final "remaining" method.

### *Why does it work?*

It waits to propose a solution, which builds trust. It makes your proposal seem like the only possible option. It makes the audience think twice about doing anything other than what you want.

### *When do you use it?*

When you want to persuade your audience to take a specific action. When there are multiple options to choose from. When the other options have problems that your option doesn't have.

———

―――

### *What is the step-by-step process?*

Option presentation: "Here's another option we could take." Option invalidation: "Here's what's wrong with that option." Repetition: repeat steps one and two for all other options. Last method presentation: "Here's the final remaining method." Last method validation: "Here's why the final method works."

Here are some guidelines: don't be too derisive of the other options. That makes it seem personal. Try your best to seem objective and logical. This is an objective and logical structure, isn't it? Go through all the other options, if possible. If not? Go through the most popular ones. Don't present your method until you've invalidated all the other options. Try to make your method seem good in the ways that the others are bad, achieving contrast persuasion.

―――

---

### 3.17: PAST, PRESENT, FUTURE

*What is it?*

Structuring a persuasive speech around the past, present, and future. Showing how a solution works not only in the present, but the past and future too.

*Why does it work?*

It makes your proposed solution seem timeless. It builds belief in your solution. It removes the common objection: "it won't work in the future," and the common objection: "it hasn't worked in the past."

*When do you use it?*

When you want to persuade your audience to accept a solution to a very consequential problem that you can't afford applying an ineffective solution to. When there is history related to your solution from which you can draw a past example. When the solution will be used for a long time, and people need to be particularly certain that it is valuable, proven, and effective.

---

___

### *What is the step-by-step process?*

Solution presentation: "Here's what we should do." The past: "Here's how this solution worked in the past, or here's how this solution would have been better than what was done." The present: "Here's why this solution is the best right now." The future: "Here's why this solution will continue to work in the future."

Here's what you're basically doing with this: asserting yourself over three dimensions of time.

Many speakers make a common mistake; the mistake of only speaking in terms of the present; of only answering the question "why does this solution work now?" With this structure, you are answering these three questions:

"Why does this solution work now?"

"Has this solution worked in the past?" "

"Will this solution work in the future?"

And here's the truth: if you can conclusively assert your ideas in the past, present, and future, you will be a lot more persuasive.

___

___

## 3.18: DESIRE, DISSONANCE, DECISION TRIFECTA

### What is it?

Structuring a persuasive speech around an unfulfilled desire. Showing your audience how they can satisfy the desire.

### Why does it work?

It puts people in a state of cognitive dissonance, and they will do anything to close the gap. It hits the pain-points of the audience over and over, and then provides an action to relieve those pain-points. It uses emotion, a powerful motivator, and it focuses on directly addressing the "WIIFM" question.

### When do you use it?

When you want to persuade your audience to make a particular decision. When your proposed action fills a desire. When your audience has an unfilled desire, that

___

you can hit upon over and over again to create powerful cognitive dissonance.

### What is the step-by-step process?

Desire: "Don't you want to [insert desire]?" Dissonance: "Right now, [insert desire] isn't real. You're missing it." Decision "Here's what you have to do to fulfill that desire."

Time to answer a million-dollar question: what do people want? You need to know this so that you can present the unfulfilled desire. And here's the short answer: survival, enjoyment of life, life extension; enjoyment of food and beverages; freedom from fear pain, and danger; sexual companionship; comfortable living conditions; to be superior, winning, keeping up with the Joneses; care and protection of loved ones; social approval.

Those are our core, evolutionary, psychological desires. They are innate. They are wired into us. They were first identified by Drew Eric Whitman in his book

———

*Cashvertising.* We also have learned desires: to be informed, satisfying curiosity, cleanliness of body and surroundings, efficiency, convenience, dependability, quality, expression of beauty and style, profit, bargains.

There are also six core drivers in our search for meaning: our drive to acquire, our drive to bond, our drive to learn, our drive to defend, our drive to feel, and our drive to improve.

# *CHAPTER FOUR*
# *INFORMATIONAL STRUCTURES*

___

## DON'T MAKE THIS MISTAKE

Have you ever listened to a speaker that has bored you for (what seemed like) hours? It's possible that your audiences feel like that about you. And I know I don't want that for myself when I'm speaking. I especially don't want that for you. These informational structures will avoid it.

But before we jump into them let me answer this question you might be asking yourself: "this is a persuasion book, what does informing people have to do with persuasion?"

And here's my answer: informing demands persuasion. You need to persuade people to opt-in, and buy-in with their mental energy and attention. You need to persuade people to listen to your information and trust you. And much of effective persuasion demands effectively informing your audience as well. Information and persuasion are inextricably tied together.

___

---

## 4.1: THE INFORMATIONAL MOTIVATED SEQUENCE

### *What is it?*

Shortening Monroe's Motivated Sequence so that each step is one sentence or a handful of sentences. Putting that before an informational speech to persuade your audience to listen to the information.

### *Why does it work?*

It provides clear, obvious benefits of listening to the speech. It avoids the mistake of forgetting to make the audience care about the information before sharing the information. It guarantees that the audience knows why the information is important and worth their time.

### *When do you use it?*

When you want to inform, but you aren't sure if the audience cares about the information. When the benefits of listening to you are not already clear. When you want to guarantee audience interest before informing. And

---

even if these things aren't true, most of the time that you need to inform, this structure works.

### What is the step-by-step process?

Attention: "Listen, you have a problem!" Need: "Here's why you need to solve this problem." Satisfaction: "This information will fix the problem. Desire: "Here's how great it will feel to know this, and the great things you can do with the information." Action: "So listen to this!" Information: Proceed with your informational speech.

This is one of my favorite structures. Why? Because it instantly applies Monroe's Motivated Sequence to an informational speech. There are four types of speeches: those to inform, persuade, inspire, and entertain. And obviously, Monroe's Motivated Sequence is persuasive. The Informational Motivated Sequence is informational. And a simple three-step process turns Monroe's Motivated Sequence to an informational structure.

Squish Monroe's Motivated Sequence until each step is one or two sentences. Put it in front of an informational speech. Enjoy more interest, attention, and applause. It is the art of using Monroe's Motivated Sequence to persuade the action of listening to your information. In other words, instead of getting right into your information, while your audience is wondering "What does this have to do with me? Why should I care? Why is this information important to me?" first, do the following…

Sentence one (attention): "It's a problem if you don't know this information." Sentence two (need): "If you don't understand this, you will [insert bad consequence one], [insert bad consequence two], [insert bad consequence three]." Sentence three (satisfaction): "But I can teach you!" Sentence four (visualization): "When you learn this, you will [insert benefit one], [insert benefit two], [insert benefit three]." Sentence five (action): "So if you give me X minutes of your time, I'll teach you everything about [subject]."

It's that simple. Only then do you get into your information. Why is this useful? Because it makes your audience care. It shows them why they should listen. It guarantees that they don't see you the same way they saw their stuffy Algebra teacher.

## 4.2: STRAIGHT-LINE METHOD
### What is it?

A speech structured around a logical progression of points, from evidence to the main claim. A speech structured as a sequence of logical units that form a straight line of claims, justifications, and evidence.

### Why does it work?

It clearly and deliberately breaks down the logic of an argument. It moves through the logic with discipline, and produces a claim from evidence (instead of fitting evidence to a claim). It makes your audience understand your logic, which leads to them accepting your claim.

―――

### When do you use it?

When you want to prove a point in the most clear, logical, and undeniable way. When you want to explain a complicated line of reasoning. When you want to inform your audience why something is true, or why something isn't true. When your audience is being driven by logic, and not emotion, or at least not *too much* emotion. Or, when you have supplied the emotional persuasion, and you need logic to give your audience permission to let their emotional hunch take the wheel.

### What is the step-by-step process?

Evidence presentation: "Here's what we know." Evidence explanation: "Here's why that evidence is significant. Here's what it really means." Logical connection: "Here's why it connects to a broader claim." Main claim presentation: "Here's the main claim. Here's the truth proven by the evidence." Run wild: run wild and explain the significance of your claim, of the truth you've discovered. You've proven it, but why does it

―――

matter? What does it mean? Why should your audience care? Now you can break away from pure reasoning and logic, and get into the personal and impactful interpretation.

If you're confused (which I totally understand), here's a basic example. Evidence: "Scientists estimate that storm damage will increase by 37% by 2025 if we don't solve climate change." Explanation of why the evidence is important: "This is important because storms cost a lot of money to repair." The connections between the evidence to a main claim: "The money comes from state emergency tax pools. But, if they run out, then states have to raise taxes, or request funds from the federal government. This leads to raised taxes on both the state and federal level. This means that climate change costs a lot of money for people. Over time, it will cost more money not to solve climate change than it will to do something about it. Solving climate change will save billions of dollars over the long run." Main claim: "Thus, we should solve climate change." Run wild:

"Ironically, the opponents of climate-change relief say that it is too expensive to fix. But, turns out fixing it costs less than not fixing it."

The straight-line structure makes you seem sharp as a tack, well-researched, logical, sophisticated, direct, and assertive. So why shouldn't you love it? Think about it: all it really is, is pushing through the muck, and using logic to connect a claim to evidence. Now, most speakers do that anyway. But here's the problem: they usually do it inside their minds and nowhere else. This is essentially taking the mental, internal logical processes that probably already occurred in your mind, and deliberately stating the logic for your audience. You might be wondering, "isn't this persuasion?" No. Arguments that are purely logical, if the logic is sound, are simply informing. Logical syllogisms, like "A equals B, and B equals C, so A equals C" are not persuasion. In other words, you're informing people why a truth is true. That's education, not persuasion.

## 4.3: REVERSE LINE METHOD

### *What is it?*

A speech structured around a logical progression of points, starting with the claim, and then connecting it to evidence.

### *Why does it work?*

It starts with the claim, which provides context for the evidence. It makes the claim when audience attention is highest: at the start. It is still a series of disciplined, logical connections, just in reverse.

### *When do you use it?*

When you want to prove a claim in a bullet-proof way. When you don't want to wait until the end of the speech to present the claim. When it would seem dishonest to go from evidence to claim, because the audience already knows what you think.

―――

### *What is the step-by-step process?*

Main claim presentation: "Here's the main claim. Here's the truth that I will prove with evidence." Logical connection: "Here's why this claim is proven by the evidence." Evidence presentation: "Here's the exact evidence that proves the claim. Here's what we know." Evidence explanation: "Here's why that evidence is significant. Here's what it really means." Run wild: run wild and explain the significance of your claim; of the truth you've discovered. You've proven it, but why does it matter? What does it mean? Why should your audience care?

Let's use the previous example from the "straight-line" approach. Main claim: "We should solve climate change." The connections between the claim to evidence: "Solving climate change will save billions of dollars over the long run. Over time, it will cost more money not to solve climate change than it will to do something about it. Climate change costs a lot of money for people. It leads to raised taxes on both the state and

―――

federal level. The money first comes from state emergency tax pools. But, if they run out, then states have to raise taxes, or request funds from the federal government." Evidence: "Scientists estimate that storm damage will increase by 37% by 2025 if we don't solve climate change." Explanation of why the evidence is important: "This is important because storms cost a lot of money to repair." Run wild: "Ironically, the opponents of climate-change relief say that it is too expensive to fix. But, turns out fixing it costs less than not fixing it."

## 4.4: STREAM OF CONSCIOUSNESS
### What is it?
Speaking in a loose stream of consciousness, structured around a particular story, theme, or idea.

### Why does it work?
It is engaging, and strengthens the speaker to audience connection. It requires much less planning than other

structures. It creates a smooth flow of information if it is executed well.

### When do you use it?

When you want to speak in a more informal way. When you feel comfortable allowing your stream of consciousness to run free. When you understand the subject-matter well enough to speak without a more defined structure, or when *you* are the subject.

### What is the step-by-step process?

Overarching theme presentation: present a central story, theme or idea. Connection presentation: present how what you're going to be talking about connects to the central story, theme, or idea. Stream of consciousness: start speaking. Connection repetition: as you speak, repeatedly tie what you're saying back to the overarching theme.

Is this even a structure? I debated that for a long time before deciding to put it in this book. Sometimes the lack of structure is, in a way, a structure. But only if you can do one thing: consistently connect what you're talking about to the central theme or idea.

For example, let's say that you are asked to speak about yourself. Maybe you're a role model for the audience. Maybe the audience is a room of interns who all want your job someday. So, the subject is your life and career. The theme is the lens through which you talk about yourself. Let's say that your theme is the qualities that led you to success: discipline, honesty, and confidence. As you're streaming out stories about your career, repeatedly connect them to that theme. Show how those qualities are a constant thread throughout your entire life.

### 4.5: MONTAGE STRUCTURE
*What is it?*
A series of stories, events, or examples that are unrelated except for their connection to a central idea.

### Why does it work?

It provides rapid-fire novelty, which captivates audiences. It uses engaging narrative, which inherently grabs attention. It presents a subtle claim, and illustrates it, rather than stating it.

### When do you use it?

When you want to almost guarantee an engaged audience. When you want to use narratives throughout your speech. When you want to illustrate, rather than flat-out state, one big central idea, and create the sense that the idea emerges as an undeniable truth from the stories.

### What is the step-by-step process?

Theme presentation: present your theme, central idea, or core message. Be brief! Don't elaborate. Just say it. Montage presentation: present your stories sequentially. After each story, briefly connect it to the theme. Montage elaboration: elaborate on how the theme exists in all of the montage stories. Theme elaboration: elaborate on the theme.

This structure works for two reasons: first, stories are naturally engaging. Second, you illustrate a theme, rather than flat out stating it. In other words, when your audience leaves, they'll deeply understand the theme on an intuitive level. Why? Because rather than telling them, you illustrated it. That is much more vivid and memorable. It prompts them to think about it and extract the theme from the stories after only a little direction with the brief theme-statement at the start. Thus, the main message is not sent into their minds from outside; rather, it emerges in their minds, from within.

This structure is also engineered for novelty. Why? Because the "montage" of the different stories provides rapid-fire information. That too is naturally engaging.

---

## 4.6: ATTACHED LIST STRUCTURE

### What is it?

A claim followed by a list of pieces of supporting evidence, sub-claims, examples, etc. Any complete statement broken down into a list of parts. A list of statements supporting one big idea.

### Why does it work?

Because it is efficient, straightforward, and avoids misunderstanding. It minimizes the need for transitions. It uses a clear and memorable list structure.

### When do you use it?

When you want to make deliberate, technical points, in a sophisticated way. When clarity is your first priority. When you want to inform about a big idea that can be broken down into sub-points, or want to provide a superabundance of proof.

---

### What is the step-by-step process?

Main idea presentation: what do all of the informational sub-units fall under? What's the big heading? The main, central principle? Sub-unit list: what are the informational sub-points that express the main idea?

Here's why this is effective: your biggest, primary focus with this structure is placed on the information.

And here's a great example. Main idea: "The United States Government is designed to create checks and balances between branches." Sub-unit list: "First form of checks and balances... second... third... fourth... etc."

Another great example? Main idea: "The minimum wage is..." Sub-unit list: "Study number one... study number two... study number three... etc."

If you're teaching and want to efficiently express a main idea, this is for you. If you want a little more "showmanship," perhaps another structure. But if you want to list out points that aren't attached to a central idea, then use this next structure.

## 4.7: DETACHED LIST STRUCTURE

### What is it?

A list of thematically related but unlinked claims. A list of information units that don't relate to one bigger idea. A list of information units that are united by quality: "interesting," "funny," or "surprising," instead of connected to a central theme.

### Why does it work?

It allows you to make multiple claims that don't support one big idea. It allows you a lot more freedom to choose your information units. It provides fast-paced novelty.

### When do you use it?

When you want to make multiple detached points that don't support one idea. When you have certain pieces of knowledge that are useful, interesting, funny, etc. and you want to teach them. When you want to inform with more freedom.

### What is the step-by-step process?

Present unifying quality: "These are some particularly hilarious pieces of information from my studies of politics." List the items: "The first funny moment... the second funny moment... the third funny moment..."

This is a fun structure. If you have a good command of the subject matter (which should always be true), this structure allows you the flexibility to put that deep, intuitive knowledge to good use.

### 4.8: INFORMATION STACK

### What is it?

Structuring your speech in a series of "information units," starting with the basic, leading to the complex, and, if possible, presenting one complete concept, idea, process, etc.

### Why does it work?

Because it is efficient. Because it guarantees that your audience understands the advanced information.

———

Because it focuses on making your audience experts in one particular subject-area.

### When do you use it?

When you are teaching a complex subject to novices. When you want to give your audience a practical, working understanding of something. When you want the audience to synthesize how all the information fits together.

### What is the step-by-step process?

Promise the outcome: "Today, I'm going to teach you exactly how to do [insert process]." Present the stack order: "First, you'll learn the basics, like [insert sub-topic]. Then, we'll move into a few expert secrets, such as [insert sub-topic]. After that, you'll learn... etc." Present the stack items: start presenting the items in the stack, from the easy to the complex.

Let me tell you a secret: almost all areas of study are like pyramids. In other words, they have a set of basic

———

concepts, which lead to more and more advanced topics up the pyramid. And if you try to start at the top of the pyramid, it will be much harder to help your audience understand these difficult concepts. So, here's how the information stack solves that problem: it forms a gentle ladder of understanding not unlike a persuasive yes-ladder. How? By first starting with the basic, easy concepts, and then stacking the advanced concepts on top of the basics. Stacking your information in this way guarantees your audience will understand the advanced concepts with greater ease and less frustration.

## 4.9: THE BIG ANSWER
### *What is it?*

Structuring your speech around a massive mental open loop. An informational speech that teases a big answer.

---

### Why does it work?

Because it is incredibly suspenseful and captivating. Because it creates curiosity, which grabs attention. Because it creates intrigue.

### When do you use it?

When you can work a "central question" into your speech. When you have a "big answer" to the central question. When you are informing an audience.

### What is the step-by-step process?

Present the subject: "Today, we're going to be talking about [insert subject]." Present the dilemma: "There's a dilemma. There's a problem with [insert subject]." Present the central question: "The big question nobody can answer is why does [the problem with your subject] keep happening? Why is [insert subject] so broken?" Tease the big answer: "I have the big answer to that big question. I'll tell you at the end of the speech." Inform: this is the bulk of your speech. Inform the audience.

---

Give the big-answer: "Remember the big question? Well, here's the answer: [insert answer]."

If you don't know what a mental "open loop" is, then you probably don't see why this structure is so powerful. A mental open loop is created, in this case, when you present the question. A question demands an answer to close the mental loop. And if you don't close the open loop, people crave to close it. The open loop is strengthened when you tell them that you have the big answer. It's strengthened even more if you tease it, saying things like "it's the most simple, unexpected answer that even experts haven't found."

Here's what the open loop does: it creates massive curiosity in your audience, it gets you audience attention, and it makes your audience sit on the edge of their seats, thinking "what's the big answer?" And here's how you can strengthen the open loop even further: repeatedly repeat the big question during the speech, and repeatedly tease the big answer during the speech. I mentioned in the foreword of this book that the foreword itself was

___

an example of structure theory in action. This was the structure I used.

## 4.10: THE BACK-AND-FORTH
### *What is it?*
Structuring your speech around a back-and-forth debate between two sides.

### *Why does it work?*
Because the back-and-forth structure builds an ongoing open loop: "who is right?" Because presenting both sides of an argument is engaging. Because the audience can decide for themselves who they agree with, and in doing so, intellectually engage themselves with the subject matter, while seeing you as an objective, logical, trustworthy person due to your impartiality.

### *When do you use it?*
When you are informing an audience about a subject that is divisive. When there are two distinct sides in argument

___

about your subject that have clear arguments in favor of their opposing stances. When you are an objective "teacher" rather than someone on one of the two sides, and your goal is to accurately represent the debate or subject area as best as you can.

### What is the step-by-step process?

Subject presentation: "Here's what we're going to be talking about." Preliminary information: "Here's what you need to know about this subject." Side presentation: "Here are the two sides. Here's how they disagree about this subject." Side one argument presentation: "Here's the first main argument of one side." Side two rebuttal: "Here's how the second side responds." Side two argument presentation: "Here's the first main argument of the second side." Side one rebuttal: "Here's how the first side responds." Back-and-forth repetition: Repeat the argument presentation and rebuttal steps for as many arguments as you want.

Rather than just informing your audience, you're engaging them in an intellectual debate. This makes them more interested, helps them remember your information, gets them thinking, and informs them better than just laying out the information ever would. You're informing through the lens of an engaging argument. Very powerful. An equally engaging (and much easier) structure is number eleven. Here it is.

## 4.11: CHRONOLOGICAL
### *What is it?*

Structuring your informational speech along the lines of a chronological sequence of events. Telling a chronological story.

### *Why does it work?*

Because the structure is straightforward and mirrors the information. Because chronological stories are engaging and provide novelty. Because it is the best way to present a sequence of events, simply due to the mirror effect between subject matter and structure that it creates.

### When do you use it?

When you are informing an audience about history, or relaying a story. When you are relaying information about a sequence of events. When your information naturally fits into a chronological structure.

### What is the step-by-step process?

Subject presentation: "Here's what I'm going to teach you about today." Chronological presentation: "First, [insert event]. Then, [insert event]. After that, [insert event] happened, etc."

Simple, but elegant. The easy part of this structure is that your information is "pre-structured" for you. Only use this when the chronological aspect of the subject matter isn't contrived. Don't try to fit a square peg into a round hole.

## 4.12: CAUSE AND EFFECT

### *What is it?*

Structuring your speech around a prominent cause and effect relationship. Presenting the cause, and then what it causes.

### *Why does it work?*

Because it focuses on the relationship between the two things. Because the cause-and-effect frame helps the audience put the information in context. Because many subjects are, in reality, split into causes and effects. Because it speaks in terms of consequences, and consequences raise the stakes of the situation, which engages.

### *When do you use it?*

When your information can be split into a set of causes, and a set of effects. When your information is about current events. When you have a specific analysis of the cause-and-effect relationship.

―――

___

### What is the step-by-step process?

Present the cause: "Here's what has been happening." Present the effect: "Here's what this has led to." Repetition: repeat the previous two steps for a series of cause-and-effect relationships related to a subject.

If you're like me, and a lot of your speeches are analyzing current events, then this structure is perfect. Why? Because this structure allows you to focus the speech on your own analysis. And if you are an expert on a subject, then that's exactly what your audience wants.

## 4.13: PRESENTATION, ESCALATION, CONTRAST TRIFECTA

### What is it?

Structuring your speech around a response to a common point of view. Structuring your speech around a "reframing" technique.

___

### *Why does it work?*

It uses reframing, which can be especially informative. It challenges an intellectual consensus. It responds to another point of view, which is engaging.

### *When do you use it?*

When you are informing about something, and there is another common opinion that happens to be wrong. When the information is primarily about the relationship between two things. When you can use frame escalation, a reframing technique.

### *What is the step-by-step process?*

Frame presentation: "Most people say that X [insert relationship] Y." Pre-escalation: "However, they're wrong. They're wrong because [insert reasons]." Frame escalation: "Actually, it turns out that X [insert different relationship] Y. Or, turns out that Y [insert original relationship] X. Or, turns out that X [opposite relationship] Y." Contrast: "While most people think,

———

[original frame], they're actually wrong. The truth is that [escalated frame]."

Here's what reframing is: changing the relationship between two subjects. (Actually, it's a bit more complex. This is just basic reframing).

For example, here are some logical relationships: X causes Y. X happens because of Y. X happens despite Y. X is necessary for Y. X is disconnected from Y. X contradicts Y

And here's what frame escalation is: zooming out on a common frame and reversing it from a new perspective. Changing the perceived relationship between two things. Controlling the narrative and the information. For example, let's say most people criticize a public figure. They say X statement contradicts Y statement. If you object to this, there are a few options: you could say the contradiction doesn't matter, or find a way to say it isn't a contradiction.

But there's one very good option: escalating the frame from an "X contradicts Y" statement, to an "X is

———

true because of Y" statement. This is at once counterintuitive and intuitive. The world's most effective politicians, and the winners of political debates, have been the ones who have used frame escalation.

Frame escalation is especially effective if the new frame and the original frame seem to be at odds with one another. In other words, frame escalation is particularly powerful, persuasive, and elegant if the new frame seems to undo, or totally reverse, the old frame, completely deflating its energy.

## 4.14: NARRATIVE STRUCTURE
### *What is it?*
Structuring your speech around a narrative story. Informing through a story.

### *Why does it work?*
It uses long-form narrative, which captivates audiences. It gets audiences wondering, "what comes next?" It builds a speaker to audience connection.

―――

### When do you use it?

When you are informing about a philosophical concept, rather than set of facts. When you can illustrate the concept through a story. When you want to "show" not "tell" the concept.

### What is the step-by-step process?

Exposition: "These are the characters and setting." Rising action: "Here's when the conflict started. Tension stared building." Climax: "This is what happened in the peak of the conflict." Falling action: "Here's what happened after the conflict. Things started to relax." Resolution: "Here's how life was different after the whole thing happened." Thematic takeaway: "Here's the theme we learn from this story."

Why is this structure so effective? Because it is naturally captivating. People love stories. But there's another element to it: it "shows" and doesn't "tell" a central message. In other words, your audience comes to the thematic takeaway themselves rather than you telling

―――

them the thematic takeaway directly. So, they feel like they truly know it. It becomes part of them. It's a conclusion they've reached themselves.

## 4.15: DEMONSTRATIVE
### *What is it?*

Structuring your speech around demonstrating the qualities of a new thing.

### *Why does it work?*

It is a simple template to demonstrate a new innovation. It describes almost everything about a new creation. It inherently contains fast-paced novelty.

### *When do you use it?*

When you are informing about something new. When you want to give people a complete picture of a new innovation. When you are presenting a new product, idea, or creation.

### What is the step-by-step process?

What it is: "Here's what we created! Check it out!" What it does: "Here's exactly what it does." How it does it: "It does it in this way." Why it's needed: "This is the problem it solves." What its benefits are: "These are the benefits it has." How it's different: "It's different from older things of the same category in these ways." Proof of concept: "Here's the proof that something of this kind works." Proof of efficacy: "Here's the proof that this specific one works." Cost framing: "It's $3,000 less than the older model." Trust indicators: "It has X positive reviews. You can trust it because [insert trust indicators]."

This one is pretty simple. Just fill in the blanks. This structure is inherently filled with novelty. People love fast-paced, new information. This structure will always give new information quickly. For this structure, make each step seem like a whole new massive reveal. That will compound its power.

## 4.16: SHORT-FORM INFORMATIONAL THREE-POINT PUNCH

### What is it?

Structuring your speech around a main piece of information and three supporting examples.

### Why does it work?

It is a brief way to teach a complete concept. It uses three examples, and you usually don't need more. It can be used for almost any information.

### When do you use it?

When you are informing an audience about anything. When you have supporting examples. When you want to inform efficiently.

### What is the step-by-step process?

Main piece of information: "The big idea is…" Example one: "The first time this was seen was…" Example two:

"Another example is…" Example three: "And another clear piece of evidence is…"

# CHAPTER FIVE
# INSPIRATIONAL STRUCTURES

———

*225*

___

**THE SCIENCE OF INSPIRATION**

This chapter will teach you exactly how to give speeches that will excite your audiences, inspire your audiences, and motivate your audiences. For example, the "want-got" structure can inspire almost any audience if you illustrate the persuasive gap correctly. But we'll talk about that later. Are you ready to get into it? Let's start.

**5.1: QUOTE PRESENTATION**

*What is it?*

Structuring a speech around the best quotes from the best experts in a subject area. Usually, the subject area is one of aspiration. The audience wants to be good at it.

*Why does it work?*

It is an easy structure because the content is already given to you. The quotes from the experts provide authority. The structure is linear and straightforward.

___

## When do you use it?

When you are inspiring an audience. When the audience is particularly interested in a subject area. When you can compile a set of quotes from experts about the subject.

## What is the step-by-step process?

Present subject: "Today, we're going to be talking about [subject area]." Present structure: "Sure, I'm pretty good at [subject area]. But today, I'm going to bring you the wisdom from the top minds on [subject area]. They have a lot more wisdom than I do." Present first expert: "[Insert expert] once said something very important about [subject area]. Here's what you need to know about [insert expert]." Present quote: "Here's what [insert expert] said." Present analysis: "Here's what this means." Repeat steps three-five: Repeat the previous three steps for as many quotes as you want.

Let me tell you why you will love this structure: you have to do almost no work. You are given instant eloquence. You are guaranteed to be giving valuable

___

___

inspiration. Just go Google "quotes about [subject]." You are guaranteed to find inspirational, eloquent, and relevant quotes you can use. If not, search for "inspirational quotes about [subject]." Select the top three most inspirational quotes, and use them with this structure. You'll save hours. And you'll instantly be eloquent because the quotes will always be well-worded. This is easy and effective.

## 5.2: LONG-FORM ANAPHORA
### *What is it?*
Structuring an entire speech around the rhetorical device anaphora.

### *Why does it work?*
It uses anaphora, a rhetorical device of repetition that is incredibly eloquent. It has been proven by the inspirational speeches recorded in history. It cements a core message through repetition.

### When do you use it?

When you have a clear purpose, you want to inspire your audience towards achieving. When your core message bears repetition. When you want to use a simple repetitive template that you can fill in.

### What is the step-by-step process?

Anaphora purpose phrase: "We will do [action]…" Subsequent clause: "…so that we can [result]. Or, another subsequent clause, like "…to [group, person, institution, etc.]" Repetition: repeat steps one and two until you have a full-length speech.

At this point you're probably very confused. I get it. First, let me define anaphora: the repetition of a word or phrase at the beginning of successive clauses.

When I discovered this inspirational speech structure, I was shocked and confused, until I found more and more examples of history's legendary leaders using it.

___

Then I realized I stumbled across something incredible. Truly incredible. Some examples follow. I've cut out everything unnecessary to our purposes. This allows us to see, clear as day, the long-form anaphora structure.

Martin Luther King: "I have a dream that one day [anaphora phrase] this nation will rise up [subsequent clause]... I have a dream that one day [anaphora phrase] on the red hills of Georgia son [subsequent clause]... I have a dream that one day [anaphora phrase] even the state of Mississippi [subsequent clause]... I have a dream that [anaphora phrase] my four little children will one day [subsequent clause]... I have a dream ... I have a dream that [anaphora phrase] one day in Alabama [subsequent clause]... I have a dream today ... I have a dream that [anaphora phrase] one day every [subsequent clause]."

Winston Churchill: "We shall [anaphora phrase] not [subsequent clause] flag or fail... We shall [anaphora phrase] go on [subsequent clause]... We shall fight [anaphora phrase] in France [subsequent clause]… We shall fight [anaphora phrase] on [subsequent clause]… We shall fight [anaphora phrase] with [subsequent clause]… We shall defend [anaphora phrase] this [subsequent clause]… We shall fight [anaphora phrase] on [subsequent clause]… We shall fight [anaphora phrase] on [subsequent clause]… We shall fight [anaphora phrase] in the [subsequent clause]… We shall fight [anaphora phrase] in the [subsequent clause]… We shall [anaphora phrase] never surrender [subsequent clause]

Bernie Sanders: this example stunned me. It is contemporary, and he moves through four different anaphora purpose phrases that dominate his speech. Remember this: anaphora purpose phrases are called so because they are often presenting a purpose. You'll see exactly that right now.

Phase one: "We say to the [anaphora phrase] private health insurance companies [subsequent clause]… Today, we say to the [anaphora phrase] pharmaceutical industry [subsequent clause]... Today, we say to [anaphora phrase] Walmart, the fast food industry and other low wage employers [subsequent clause]... Today we say to [anaphora phrase] corporate America [subsequent clause]... Today we say to [anaphora phrase] the American people that [subsequent clause]... Today we say to [anaphora phrase] the parents in this country that [subsequent clause]... Today, we say to [anaphora phrase] our young people that [subsequent clause]... Today, we say to [anaphora phrase] our senior citizens, that [subsequent clause]... Today, we say to [anaphora phrase] Donald Trump and the fossil fuel industry that [subsequent clause]... Today, we say to [anaphora phrase] the prison-industrial-complex that [subsequent clause]... Today, we say to [anaphora phrase] the American people that [subsequent clause]... Today, we say to [anaphora phrase] the top 1 percent and the large profitable corporations in this country – people who have never had it so good — that [subsequent clause]... Today, we say to [anaphora phrase] the military-industrial-complex that [subsequent clause]

Phase two: "I did not come from [anaphora phrase] [subsequent clause]... I did not come from [anaphora phrase] [subsequent clause]... I did not come from [anaphora phrase] [subsequent clause]

Phase three: "Together [anaphora purpose phrase], as billionaires and large corporations have [subsequent clause]... Together [anaphora purpose phrase], as the forces of militarism have [subsequent clause]... Together [anaphora purpose phrase], as so many of our young people have [subsequent clause]."

Phase four: "When we are in the White House, we will [anaphora phrase] enact [subsequent clause]... When we are in the White House we will [anaphora phrase] attack [subsequent clause]... When we are in the White House we will [anaphora phrase] end [subsequent clause]... When we are in the White House, we will [anaphora phrase] move [subsequent clause]... When we are in the White House, we are going to [anaphora purpose phrase] address… When we are in the White House, we are going to [anaphora phrase] protect [subsequent clause]

Entire speeches, world-changing speeches, nation-moving speeches, have been constructed with this process: an anaphora phrase, a subsequent clause, repetition of steps one and two, and, if needed, a new anaphora purpose phrase, repeating steps two and three.

Want to see how powerful this structure is? Check it out: both Winston Churchill and Martin Luther King's speeches are referred to by their anaphora purpose phrase. Churchill's is called his "we shall fight speech." MLK's is called his "I have a dream speech."

And consider how the anaphora purpose phrase lines up with the actual purpose of the speech.

For Churchill, his purpose was to inspire the United Kingdom to fight. His anaphora purpose phrase was "we shall fight."

For MLK, his purpose was to inspire the African American community and the civil rights movement to

___

dream. His anaphora purpose phrase was "I have a dream."

Bernie Sanders had multiple purposes: inspiring people to speak out against power, inspiring people to embrace where they came from, inspiring people to come together, and inspiring people to take the White House by voting for him.

Look at his anaphora purpose phrases: "Today, we say to... I did not come from... Together... When we are in the White House..."

Look at how they line up with his purposes: "Today, we say to... (inspiring people to speak out against power) I did not come from... (inspiring people to embrace where they came from) Together... (inspiring people to come together) When we are in the White House (inspiring people to take the White House by voting for him)..."

That's why I call it an "anaphora *purpose* phrase." It almost always lines up directly to the purpose of the speech.

___

___

### 5.3: WANT, GOT, EMPOWERMENT
*What is it?*

Structuring a speech around presenting a gap between what people want and what they have. Then, inspiring them to close that gap.

*Why does it work?*

It uses the aspirations of the audience. It creates cognitive dissonance. It makes the "empowerment" actually make sense in the context of the gap.

*When do you use it?*

When your audience has a clear gap in their lives that could be filled. When you want to inspire your audience. When you want to empower them to close the "want-got" gap.

*What is the step-by-step process?*

Want presentation: "Here's what you want to have in your life." Got presentation: "Instead, here's what you

___

———

actually have. It's not what you want." Want-got repetitive contrast: repeatedly jump back and forth, contrasting what they want with what they have. Empowerment: "But you can get what you want. You have what it takes."

I told you that there would be a lot of contrast persuasion and aspirational persuasion. This speech structure uses both. A common mistake speakers make when trying to inspire is *just doing the empowerment*. But the empowerment becomes a lot more useful in the context of a want-got gap. I'll repeat something: a solution only makes sense in the context of a problem.

## 5.4: PRESENT PROBLEMS, FUTURE, EMPOWERMENT TRIFECTA
### *What is it?*

Structuring a speech around the problems of the present, and then empowering the audience to fix them in the future.

———

### Why does it work?

It contrasts a problematic present with a better future. It puts the empowerment in context. It presents a vision for the future.

### When do you use it?

When you want to inspire your audience to work towards a better future. When there are problems in the present that your audience is struggling with. When you want to be a visionary or a leader.

### What is the step-by-step process?

Current problems: "Here's what's wrong right now." Future vision: "Here's how the future can look. Here's how it can feel to pass these obstacles." Empowerment: "You can do it. You can make this difference. You have the power."

Simple, but elegant. Here's a tip: it's important to have specific, symmetric contrast. Here's a contrast between present and future that is neither specific nor symmetric: "Our business processes are inefficient and frustrating. We can have better management."

Here's why it satisfies neither of the two criteria: "business processes" is a vague phrase, and "business processes" and "better management" are not symmetric. In other words, the future must be good in the same way, along the same dimension, that the present is bad.

Here's a contrast between present and future that is both specific and symmetric. "Our sales processes are inefficient and frustrating. We can have streamlined, satisfying, rewarding sales processes." In this example, the speaker is pointing out a specific problem in the present. In the future, it is this same specific problem that is fixed.

___

## 5.5: SHORT-FORM INSPIRATIONAL THREE-POINT PUNCH

### What is it?

Structuring a speech around examples of your audience having the qualities they need to have to do what they want.

### Why does it work?

It makes your audience feel like they are capable. It makes your audience confident in their abilities. It builds the speaker to audience connection.

### When do you use it?

When you have personal knowledge of your audience. When you know of examples of your audience expressing the necessary qualities. When you want to inspire a specific group of people to believe they can do a specific thing.

---

### *What is the step-by-step process?*

Limited frame presentation: "You might think that you aren't capable of achieving [goal]." Goal presentation: "Here's the specific goal you want to achieve. You think you can't." Qualities presentation "Here are the qualities you need to achieve that goal. You already have these qualities." Example one: "Here's the first time you showed me you have these qualities." Example two: "Here's the second time you showed me you have these qualities." Example three: "Here's the third time you showed me you have these qualities."

To summarize this structure, you're basically saying "you have everything you need to do what you want to do." In other words, you're taking a goal your audience thought was unreachable, and putting it within reach. How? By showing them extremely specific examples that prove how they *already have* exactly what it takes. In doing so, this structure removes a limiting belief (or multiple limiting beliefs).

---

―――

## 5.6: LIMITING BELIEF PREDICTION

### *What is it?*

Structuring a speech around addressing and removing your audience's limiting beliefs.

### *Why does it work?*

It makes your audience realize their own potential. It destroys their excuses. It gets rid of all their barriers to motivation.

### *When do you use it?*

When you have a solid understanding of your audience's limiting beliefs. When you want to inspire people to do something difficult. When people have lots of excuses why they won't do it.

### *What is the step-by-step process?*

Present limiting belief or excuse: "You say you can't do it because [insert limiting belief or excuse]." Invalidate limiting belief or excuse: "Here's why that limiting belief

―――

———

makes no sense." Repetition: Repeat steps one and two for all limiting beliefs your audience has. Enumeration: "Clearly all of your excuses are invalid." Empowerment: "There's nothing holding you back. The reasons you tell yourself you can't do this don't apply. You can do this."

You're systematically and repetitively invalidating your audience's limiting beliefs. You're calling them out. You're exposing their excuses. And this is often exactly what people need to be inspired.

## 5.7: VISIONARY STRUCTURE
### *What is it?*
Structuring a speech around a bright vision of the future.

### *Why does it work?*
It motivates people to strive towards that vision. It makes you a leader. It gives people a goal, and your audience can't be motivated or inspired without a goal.

———

—

### When do you use it?

When you have a bright, ambitious vision for the future. When you know your audience would appreciate your vision. When you want to inspire your audience to strive toward your vision.

### What is the step-by-step process?

Empowerment: "You are all brilliant, capable people. You all have what it takes to go after your goals." Accomplishment enumeration: "Look at all the amazing things you've already achieved. [Insert accomplishment one], [insert accomplishment two], [insert accomplishment three]." Pre-accomplishment recall: "Remember how we felt before those accomplishments? We thought we couldn't do it. But we kept working towards it, and we did it." Vision: "And now, we're turning to a new goal. [Insert your vision]." Empowerment: "We have everything it takes to go after this vision and get it." Accomplishment string: "Just like we achieved [insert accomplishment one], [insert

—

accomplishment two], and [insert accomplishment three], we will also achieve [insert your vision]."

I love this speech structure. It's basically guaranteed to move your audience towards your vision. Why? Because it doesn't just lay out your vision, leaving people wondering "how are we going to do it?" Instead, it makes the vision seem believable, and it does this because it empowers. It uses previous accomplishments to prove that the empowerment is more than just empty words. It uses the now-proven empowerment to inspire the audience to move toward the vision.

## 5.8: DRAMA STRUCTURE
### *What is it?*
Structuring a speech around an inspirational story.

### *Why does it work?*
It enthralls people. It uses narrative, which is naturally engaging. It helps people draw inspiration from another person's story.

___

### When do you use it?

When you want to inspire an audience. When you have an inspirational story related to the subject. When you have a personal background that is inspirational.

### What is the step-by-step process?

Exposition: "These are the characters and setting." Problem: "This the immense problem and the impassable obstacle the character faced." False-starts: "This is the series of failed attempts to solve the problem the character went through." Low-point: "This is the low point the character reached, when he was about to give up for good." Rising action: "Instead of giving up, he decides to try one more solution." Climax: "This was the crucial breaking point. This was when the solution either worked or failed." Success: "It worked! Here's how that felt, and what that meant for the characters." Falling action: "Here's what happened after the climax. Things started to relax." Resolution: "Here's how life was different after the whole thing happened."

Inspirational takeaway: "Here are the inspirational lessons we can take from this story."

The inspirational stories that dominate history all follow this pattern. Blockbuster inspirational movies that hit the top of the charts follow this pattern. Why shouldn't an inspirational speech follow this pattern too?

**CHAPTER SIX**
**ADVANCED TECHNQUES**

---

## 6.1: DON'T BURY THE LEAD (OR DO...)

Have you noticed that news reports immediately start with the main events? The big ideas? The primary news? That's called starting with the lead. Why am I talking about journalism? I'll explain.

The whole point of speech structure is breaking down your speech into units and ordering them to achieve a desired impact. You're with me so far, right? Each of these "sub-units" have one main idea. You can usually summarize it in one sentence. This one sentence is the "lead." It's a one-sentence summary of the entire "sub-unit," which is usually a paragraph.

And there are two strategies: you can *not* bury the lead. You can start each sub-unit with the lead. Here's what that does: it grabs attention, puts the rest of the paragraph in context, primes the audience for the rest of the information, and gives the main information when audience attention is at the highest.

So, "don't bury the lead." Or, maybe, *do* bury the lead. Because if you put the lead at the end of a sub-unit, here's what that does: it makes the lead seem like a natural conclusion of what came before it, gradually builds up to the lead (the lead emerges from the information), creates curiosity and suspense throughout the sub-unit, and acts as a closing summary before moving on to the next phase of your communication.

You have two choices. Pick one. They are both effective, but one likely suits you, your message, and your situation more than the other.

**6.2: VERSATILITY**

All of these structures can be used in multiple ways. And that's important to know. You can adapt them for different purposes. You can morph them to completely new purposes.

**6.3: LENGTHENING AND SHORTENING**

This (and the next expert technique) are the *two most powerful structure techniques*, especially when used together. Each of these structures act as an *accordion*. They can be lengthened or shortened, while retaining much of their original qualities in proportion to how much they are lengthened or shortened.

For example:, the problem-solution structure can be two sentences. Sentence one presents a problem, and sentence two presents the solution.

The gain, logic, fear trifecta can be shortened to three sentences. Sentence one presents a gain, sentence two justifies it with logic, and sentence three creates a fear of losing it.

So, here's the big secret: while all of these speech structures are designed to be entire speeches, they can all be shortened until each step of the structure is one sentence, and arguably even further than that. In other words, you can use a problem-solution structure that is an entire speech. You can use 20 sentences to describe the problem, and 20 sentences to describe the solution. But you can also make a problem-solution structure that is two sentences and has the same impact on a smaller scale. Wonderful.

### 6.4: COMBINING

You can use all of these structures in a single speech. Stretched out to full length, each of the structures is an entire speech. Condensed, you can basically use all 43 of these structures in a single speech. Now I don't recommend that you do that. Why? That might be a little much. However, I do recommend you create a speech that is a combined amalgamation of some of these structures if it suits you. Use them as building blocks to build a unique, customized tower. Just know this: because all of these structures have the same effect on a smaller scale when each step is just one sentence as they do when they are full-length, you can create incredibly complex, powerful combinations of these structures.

Just a quick example: a three-sentence past-present-means to build curiosity, with vague "means." A three-sentence diagnose, problem, solution structure, addressing the problem presented in the "past" stage of the previous structure, and now elaborating upon the solution. An objection prediction where each objection gets one sentence. This structure addresses the objections to the solution presented in the diagnose-problem-solution structure. Lastly, a tension-desire-action trifecta (three sentences, one sentence each step) to use emotional hot buttons for a final call to action.

See what I mean? I've given you 43 building blocks. The kinds of speeches you can build with them are endless. You can write a speech that's just a sequence of all 18 persuasive structures if the situation calls for it. First of all, the speech is then basically written for you (just go look at the step-by-step processes). Second of all, the persuasive punch you get from that is huge.

## 6.5: SEPARATION OF CONCERNS

I predict that a lot of people will make the same mistake: blending the different stages of the structures. Here's why that's bad: each step is designed to have a purpose, which makes sense in the sequence of steps that come before and after, and in the sequence of purposes those steps accomplish. So, when you blend them, you blur the

———

clarity of your message, you confuse your audience (and yourself), and you neuter the impact of the structure.

Here's an example: let's say you're using the past-present-means persuasive structure. Each step has a distinct purpose. If you blur them together, that purpose is lost. The whole point of the past and present steps is to create suspense and curiosity for the means that took you from the difficult past to the successful present. In other words, the past-present-means structure will drive your speech to success with an engine of curiosity and suspense. But if you blend the steps (even a little) and reveal the means before the proper time, you completely lose the suspense and curiosity. So, the whole thing becomes useless. Enter the solution: separation of concerns.

This means following a set of guidelines. These guidelines guarantee that your structure is executed properly, without blurring the steps.

The guidelines are as follow. Each step of a speech structure should be distinct. Each step of a speech

———

structure should be easily distinguishable from the others (which doesn't mean they shouldn't flow smoothly into and out of each other). Each step of a speech structure should fulfill its individual purpose before trying to do anything else (and once it does, probably leave it at that instead of trying to do something else). Each step of a speech structure should fulfill its own purpose, and not the purpose designed for another step. In other words: there's a place for everything, and everything should be in its place.

## CONCLUSION

Thank you for trusting me and reading this book. Thank you for giving me the cherished gift of communicating these ideas to you. Thank you for making it possible for me to write about the subject I love for a living.

I hope we have connected through these pages. And I am filled with gratitude, because to me, we have.

I hope these pages served you and helped you accomplish one of the most worthwhile goals: becoming an infinitely more effective communicator by learning the little-known but deeply powerful theories of masterful influence, as well as proven, step-by-step structures that change minds, inspire, and inform.

I hope you trust me when I tell you that there is no final destination; there is no stopping point, only constant improvement. You must practice this critical skill of communication every single day, because it is a gift to mankind.

We have a special, sacred, unique gift – the gift of spoken word, of connection through airwaves – and we must use it. We must not let it rust away and whither, but exercise it day in and day out.

Through this gift, we can stop or start any mass movement that ripples throughout history long after we leave this Earth.

Through this gift, we can chart a course for our lives and follow it with renewed vigor and greater potential.

Through this gift, we can make the most of this life we've been given and help others do the same.

Through this gift, we can inundate the minds of our fellow humans with ideas that are bold, brave, valuable, and viciously worthwhile; we can break through the barrier that stands between what we want and what we have, by forming big, valiant coalitions of the convinced.

It is not a question of *if* you will speak, or even of *when*, but of *how*. Will you wield a polished, poised, and precise tool, or one that is dead, degraded, and dulled from the disgrace of disuse?

Will your words be believed, or tossed aside?

Alive with potential, or dead on arrival?

Heeded, or ignored?

Credible, or incredible?

If I've accomplished my goal, you didn't have to think about those questions before you knew the answers. Thank you for letting me try. I hope I've succeeded, just as I hope that you will.

Sincerely, Peter – your partner in striving for success, for the love of the journey, not the destination.

FREE RESOURCES AVAILABLE AT
www.publicspeakinghub.com/free-resources

Made in the USA
Coppell, TX
15 February 2022

73607040R00144